With a love song floating in the background, Elizabeth turned to Michael, her eyes filling with tears.

"Michael, I love you. Maybe I don't remember much about my life before the accident, but I know that I loved you then, and I love you now."

Michael pulled her into his arms, not caring that they were standing in a busy hotel in Cancún. A memory had come back to her, a memory of their love. In time, all the memories would come back, the amnesia would clear. That was his hope, his constant prayer.

He kissed her lips and smoothed her hair back from her face. "It's going to be okay, Elizabeth. God has given us a love that will see us through the hardships. We're going to make it."

And he felt that they would, despite a killer stalking them and danger lurking at every turn. They would make it.

A PALISADES CONTEMPORARY ROMANCE

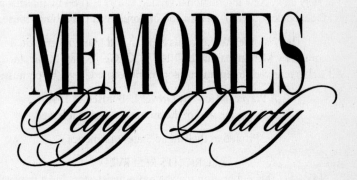

MEMORIES

Peggy Darty

PALISADES®

MEMORIES
published by Palisades
a division of Multnomah Publishers, Inc.

©1998 by Peggy Darty
International Standard Book Number: 1-57673-171-5

Cover illustration by C. Michael Dudash
Design by Brenda McGee

Scripture quotations are from:
The Holy Bible, New International Version © 1973, 1984 by International Bible Society, used by permission of Zondervan Publishing House.

"The Way We Were," words by Alan and Marilyn Bergman music by Marvin Hamlisch © 1973 COLGEMS-EMI Music, Inc. All rights reserved. International copyright secured. Used by permission.

"A Prayer to God" by Grover L. Byrdsell © 1998
Used by permission of the author. All rights reserved.

Printed in the United States of America

For information:
MULTNOMAH PUBLISHERS, INC.•POST OFFICE BOX 1720
SISTERS, OREGON 97759

Library of Congress Cataloging-in-Publication Data:
Darty, Peggy.
  Memories / by Peggy Darty.
      p. cm.   ISBN 1-57673-171-5 (alk. paper)   I. Title.
  PS3554.A79M4 1998   97-44218   813'.54—dc21   CIP

98 99 00 01 02 03 04 — 10 9 8 7 6 5 4 3 2 1

Lovingly dedicated to my readers,
who send cards and write letters of encouragement,
and in general keep me going.
Without you, there would be no book.

ACKNOWLEDGMENTS

Grateful appreciation to Hal Leonard Corporation for the use of that wonderful song, "The Way We Were."

Another note of appreciation to Grover L. Byrdsell for the use of his poem, "A Prayer to God," from his book, *Something for the Heart.*

Special thanks to Jennifer Brooks, my editor, and Michael Dudash, the gifted artist who puts his magic touch to the covers of my books.

And thank you, Linda Heard, for praying me through all my books. You're a real soul mate!

"…*being confident of this, that he who began a good work in you will carry it on to completion until the day of Christ Jesus.*"

PHILIPPIANS 1:6

ONE

Elizabeth steered her white Honda Accord from Peachtree Boulevard down a side street, then another, into a small neighborhood where a quaint Italian restaurant nestled at the end of the block. It was one of her favorite restaurants, and she was meeting Michael here at six-thirty. That would give them enough time for a quiet dinner together before their weekly meeting with their Christian counselor.

Since both their schedules were hectic, it had been difficult to arrange an appointment during the day. When Mrs. Williams had offered to baby-sit Katie on Thursday evenings, Dr. Harrison had graciously agreed to meet with them at eight o'clock each week.

"Believe me, I don't mind working one evening a week," the counselor had countered their apologies. "I enjoy the satisfaction of watching two people strengthen their marriage. And I made a promise to God," he had added with a twinkle in his eye. "If he would get me through that last year of school and help me pay off my college loans, I'd help every person who needed me."

"We definitely need you," Michael had said, shaking his hand again, while Elizabeth had thanked him.

Elizabeth was thinking about these special Thursday evenings as she turned into the driveway of the restaurant and circled to the parking lot in the rear. The restaurant was not as crowded on Thursday evenings, probably because people were staying at home before the weekend festivities began. There were several cars parked in the designated Visitors area, but she easily located an empty space in the last slot of the front row.

She backed in so she was facing the driveway and the back of the building. This way it would be easier to watch for Michael.

Glancing at her watch, she noticed she was ten minutes early. She was glad; this had been one of the areas she was trying to strengthen in her personal life. Her tendency to run late had always bothered Michael, who liked being on time. For the past four months, she had made a point of allowing herself an extra thirty minutes so that she was always on time—and sometimes early. Like this evening.

She smiled to herself as she turned the key in the ignition, cutting the engine of the car. It was a pleasant evening, with winter giving way to the first warm days of spring.

Glancing around the parking lot, Elizabeth noticed she was the only patron waiting in a car. That was okay. It would give her a few minutes to unwind from a busy day and relax while waiting for Michael.

She nestled her blonde head against the seat, crossing her hands over her pink linen pants suit. She was happier than ever. Michael had moved his office to Marietta and was living at Oak Shadows with Elizabeth and Katie. Their reunion had been a growing process for both of them, but it was well worth the effort. Their lives were filled with joy now, and even Katie was ecstatic.

Elizabeth's thoughts drifted like fireflies in the twilight. She mentally ran down her list of counseling clients, which had tripled since she first set up shop at the family plantation. She thought back to the dreadful day she had found Julie in her pool house, at the brink of suicide. Just as she talked Julie out of taking her life, Michael arrived to offer support. Julie had phoned her just last week from the clinic. Speaking in a calm, tranquil voice, she thanked Elizabeth for all she had done.

The sound of voices in the distance pulled Elizabeth back

to the present. A woman and a handsome little boy were crossing the parking lot to their car. Elizabeth smiled, watching them get into their car. She and Michael had discussed having another child. She suspected Michael would like to have a son, although he claimed he would be pleased with another little girl.

A screech of brakes interrupted her daydreams. She spotted a sleek black Jaguar rounding the corner of the restaurant. No one should be speeding like that around a blind corner. Then there was another screech of brakes in the opposite direction.

Elizabeth whirled in her seat. The woman and little boy had pulled out of a space from the back row and were heading directly into the path of the Jaguar. Anticipating what was about to happen, Elizabeth jumped out of her car and yelled to the driver to slow down. But her warning was too late. The Jaguar plowed into the driver's side of the modest Ford with a sickening crunch of metal. The young woman's features contorted with horror as she screamed and fought the wheel of the car. The little boy lurched back and forth against the seat belt as the car spun around and lunged toward the brick wall. Elizabeth started toward the vehicles, and the images became a blur as she began to run, her eyes darting from one car to the other.

"Call 911," she yelled to the driver of the Jaguar. But the car was merely idling; the man had not stopped the car to get out.

She spun around, realizing that the car was attempting to leave.

"Stop!" Elizabeth yelled. When he did not, she ran toward the back of his car, determined to get the number on his plate. Suddenly the brakes slammed again, the car backed up, and Elizabeth was gazing into the face of a man she recognized, only there was something different about him.

11

His eyes held the glaze of one not completely aware of what he had done. And then there was a flash of recognition on his face as he looked at Elizabeth. The Jaguar plowed forward again, as though both Elizabeth and he were unaware that she was standing in the edge of the drive. The right fender grazed her side, tossing her back against the concrete as though she were a rag doll.

A back door of the restaurant flew open and two men in white aprons ran out. For a moment each man froze, taking in the sight of a blonde woman in pink crumpled on the pavement and another car smashed against the brick wall. As they stared in shock, the Jaguar was merely a black streak around the far side of the restaurant and into the traffic heading toward Peachtree Boulevard.

Michael tried to tactfully wind up the conversation with the mayor as he studied the picture on his desk that always brought a little grin to his mouth.

He, Elizabeth, and Katie had gone to a studio to have some pictures made to celebrate their reunion. The picture was recent, and Elizabeth's brown eyes glowed with happiness, while Katie's face held the natural, sweet beauty that enchanted everyone she met. Michael looked like a doting father, only he thought he looked younger than the reflection that had greeted him in the mirror last fall, when the burden of their separation showed in the droop of his mouth and the dull, weary gaze in his eyes. This picture radiated the happiness they all felt. He lifted his arm to glance at his watch.

Oops, he was going to be late.

"Excuse me, sir," he said at the first opening, "but I'm meeting my wife for dinner and then we have an appointment.

Quite all right." Michael stood, cradling the phone against his shoulder while his hands flew over his desk, tidying the mess.

"Pleasure talking with you, and I'll look forward to that dinner. Thanks for calling."

He hung up the phone and grabbed his coat from the back of his chair. He raced through the offices, turning off lights and ignoring the ringing telephone. He was taking no more calls. His family now took priority over work.

He jumped into his Blazer, turned the key in the ignition, and angled his way through the traffic toward the restaurant. He picked up speed, cutting down side streets, nearing the restaurant. When he saw Elizabeth and explained his being late was because of the mayor—

He frowned as he turned into the last side street and saw the commotion at the end of the block. A fire truck was exiting the side driveway of Nick's restaurant while two police cars blocked traffic, their lights flashing. A small crowd was gathered out in front of the building, staring toward the back parking lot. The area of concern was obviously in the rear. He pulled into the driveway of Nick's house and ran across the front yard.

Elizabeth.

Where was she?

As he approached the restaurant, Nick emerged from the hovering strangers. Michael's greeting froze on his lips as he watched Nick's expression turn from a startled question mark to a scowl of dark fear. He broke into a run toward Michael.

"Thank God you're here." Nick grabbed his arm, pulling him through the crowd. "What are you looking at?" he snapped at a gawker.

Something Michael did not want to consider hovered in the back of his consciousness, a dark, terrible thought he refused to acknowledge. He was a detective; Nick needed him for someone. But as they turned the corner, Michael felt a wave of shock sweep over him; the shock built to horror, then crashed into a sickening reality.

He felt himself sway against Nick's burly side as his eyes flew to the closest ambulance, the slim body on the stretcher, the blonde head streaked with blood.

"Elizabeth!" he croaked, trying to run, yet feeling as though his knees would buckle.

He had surveyed many crime scenes in his career as a detective, but he had always been the strong one. Now, the woman he loved with all his heart and soul was the victim, and if not for Nick's strong hand, he would have fainted onto the pavement that was stained with her blood.

TWO

L ater, Michael would remember the horrible events in a blur: the paramedics hovering over Elizabeth in the back of the ambulance; the driver calling ahead to the nearest hospital as he skillfully maneuvered the speeding ambulance through the six o'clock traffic; Michael in the front seat, paralyzed with fear while a million thoughts flew around his brain. And through it all, the wail of the siren splitting the tranquillity of a soft spring night in the suburbs of Atlanta.

While they raced into Emergency with Elizabeth, Michael had mechanically given a receptionist the necessary information—name, address, insurance details. Then a kind nurse had led him to a private phone and he had managed one call to Jay, relating what little he knew of the accident. When Jay asked whom he should call, Michael began to ramble, unable to stop. The panic kept building in his mind and overflowing into his voice. He tried to concentrate. He should be the one to tell Katie. But the baby-sitter must stay until someone—Mom— could get there and take over. And someone had to locate Elizabeth's mother. Where was she? London? His mind was a blur. He had voiced these jumbled thoughts to Jay, who listened carefully and reassured him.

"Tracy and I will take care of everything," Jay promised. "Just stay with Elizabeth, and we'll be there soon."

And so Michael had stayed. And waited. It seemed an eternity before the doctor called his name and stepped quickly to his side.

"Your wife is badly bruised along her right arm and hip, but fortunately there are no broken bones. She does have a concussion, a serious one," he added gently. "If she comes out of the coma within the next twenty-four hours, we believe she'll survive. She's lost blood, but not enough to warrant a transfusion."

Michael tried to follow the doctor's words…bruises and cuts…a blow to the back of the head. And no, Michael could not see her yet. As soon as she was taken to the ICU he would be notified.

Michael sank back into the chair, staring into space, seeing nothing. All he could think about was the horrible sentence the doctor had spoken.

"*If* she comes out of the coma…" He had accented the *if*, Michael remembered. "…believe she will survive…."

He dropped his head in his hands and began to pray. *Please, Lord, make Elizabeth be all right. Make her all right.*

Sometime later, he was vaguely aware of a man taking a seat beside him, gently touching his shoulder. With glazed eyes he looked into the face of a detective he knew and merely nodded his hello. Another man stood nearby, wearing a badge clipped to his belt and a holstered gun at his side.

"Michael, I'm Tom Robinson," the man seated beside him began.

Michael nodded. "I know. I remember you. Hello, Tom."

"How is she?"

Michael drew a ragged breath. "In a coma…." Then he remembered the other ambulance and frowned at Tom. "Who else…?"

"Another woman and a little boy." Tom dropped his head.

Michael knew the answer to his question before he asked it; he could tell by the sadness in Tom's face.

"And?" Michael prompted.

He shook his head. "Neither survived."

Michael's breath caught as a horrible pain shot through his head. He couldn't bear to think about Elizabeth being another casualty. He couldn't think of anything beyond what Tom had just said to him.

"Michael, the incident occurred in the parking lot behind the restaurant, as you know," Tom said in a low, gentle voice.

Michael didn't want to hear any more, but he knew Tom had to do his job.

Tom cleared his throat and continued. "Since the restaurant's exit drive passed only one window, we have only a vague description of the other car involved."

Slowly, Michael's instincts as a detective began to revive. He had taken a quick look at the accident scene, figured someone had run over Elizabeth and wrecked against the brick wall. But now Tom was talking about *another* car. Michael focused on the young man beside him—thirties, pleasant looking, intense dark eyes. He was a good detective, according to Jay.

"Michael," Tom continued, "an older woman seated at the table by the window saw a black car drive past the window. This was only a few seconds after hearing the screech of brakes and the sound of metal crunching metal. All she can tell us is that it was a black sports car. She didn't see the driver or get the license number."

For the first time, Michael was piecing together what actually must have happened. He stared in disbelief at Tom. "Are you telling me this was a hit-and-run?"

Tom nodded. "From the looks of the tire tracks, the other car was hit, skidded into the brick wall, and somehow Elizabeth was involved. She must have been crossing the parking lot. We won't know what happened until we can talk with her."

Talk with her. What if they were never able to talk with her? A seed of anger had just been planted in Michael's stunned brain, and now the seed took root, sprouted, and budded into fury. What kind of monster would cause such an accident, then flee the scene? A dozen curses zipped through his brain, but the only word that came out of his lips was, "*Murderer.*"

"Yes, the guy's a murderer. And believe me, we have men questioning every restaurant patron, every person on the street, all the houses and establishments within the next two blocks. We'll soon have a better description of the car and driver. We'll find him, Michael. Just take care of Elizabeth," he said emphatically.

Michael stared into the man's face, hearing more than sympathy in his voice. Concern. A warning? Suddenly it hit him full force: If the driver of the other car got away without a witness, then it was quite likely that Elizabeth was the only one who could identify him.

"We're leaving a policeman here," Tom said in a calm, deliberate tone. "The hospital will be kept under surveillance."

Michael found his voice. "So what you're telling me is that my wife's life is in double danger. Not just from the accident itself but now from the lousy—"

"I don't want to give you more cause for worry," Tom interrupted. "It's quite likely that Elizabeth didn't see him, or if she did, would be unable to help us. We just don't know. Until we do, we're keeping her safe."

Michael chewed his lip as he mulled over Tom's words. "He wouldn't come here," Michael said, trying to analyze the situation. It was difficult to be objective. "At this very moment, he's putting as much distance as possible between himself and the crime scene." He grabbed Tom's arm. "You have to find him right away. The first hours are crucial."

Tom nodded. "I know. Will you contact us as soon as Elizabeth is able to talk?"

Michael nodded. "Sure, but…" He heaved a deep sigh. "Let's just pray that will be soon." He was thinking about what the doctor had told him, but Tom interpreted his meaning as something to do with finding the driver.

"We'll do all we can, Michael." He placed his hand on Michael's shoulder, as though to reassure him. Then he and his partner walked swiftly from the waiting room.

Michael watched them go, then turned and scanned the waiting room. For the first time he observed the people around him. A middle-aged couple sat at a distance, paying no attention to him. The man was comforting the woman as she cried softly into a handkerchief. Three guys in their early twenties were shuffling around in the far corner. They were young and clean cut; they looked harmless and were probably waiting on news from a friend. Otherwise, the waiting room was empty.

He was about to get up and patrol the hall to check the other waiting rooms when he heard steps rapidly approaching and spotted Jay and Tracy. They were both wearing jeans and T-shirts and looked distraught. Tracy was six months pregnant, and her belly already looked huge for her slim frame. Her eyes were red and her face was pale. She clutched Jay's hand as they rushed to Michael's side.

Jay, the younger brother who had always leaned on Michael, now provided the strong arms, the steady embrace. Michael could not speak for a moment as both Jay and Tracy put their arms around him. Tracy was making a valiant effort not to cry, but Michael could feel her shoulders gently shaking in soft, muffled sobs.

Gently, Michael pulled back and faced his brother. Jay was a couple of inches shorter than Michael, but tonight he seemed more strong and capable than anyone else. Jay's eyes held the sheen of tears, but he was trying to blink them away. Michael swallowed hard and looked down into Tracy's wet face. "Tracy, you shouldn't be here," Michael said gently. "The baby—"

"Of course I should be here!" Tracy argued.

She was as stubborn as ever, Michael thought, hugging her gently and appreciating her even more.

"Michael, have you spoken with the doctor?" Jay asked as they took a seat, Jay on one side of him, Tracy on the other.

"Yes." Michael sank back into the chair. Briefly, he related to Jay and Tracy what the doctor had told him. From the corner of his eye, he saw Tracy's hand fly to her mouth to suppress another sob.

"I've called Mom and Dad," Jay said, drawing a deep breath. "They're on their way to Oak Shadows now. Mom knew she was needed there with Katie. Dad will probably get back in his pickup and barrel down here."

Michael shook his head. "He doesn't need to sit around here. There's nothing he can do. There's nothing *I* can do but wait."

No one spoke for several seconds as Jay put a comforting hand on Michael's shoulder. The three of them sat staring at the floor, lost in their own thoughts.

Tracy broke the silence. "I'll be in charge of trying to reach Elizabeth's mother if you can tell me where to look for a telephone number."

Michael drew a deep breath, blinked a tear from his eye, and tried to think. "Elizabeth received a letter from her mother a couple of days ago. The letter may still be in her desk at home. Or maybe in the bedside table."

Jay turned to Tracy. "Mom can find it."

"They were in…London, I think," Michael said, running a hand through his hair, tousling it even more. His head felt as though two fists were pounding his temples. "I remember

Elizabeth commenting on the hotel, but I don't recall the name of it."

"There's a phone over there." Jay pointed.

"I'll call now," Tracy nodded, glancing at the phone. She pressed her hands against the arm of the chair and pushed herself up.

Jay put an arm around her, balancing her as she turned and studied Michael.

"Michael, I have some aspirin in my purse if you need one," she said, looking at him with concern.

He nodded that he did, and she dug into her huge shoulder bag and pulled out a small bottle of generic aspirin. She removed the cap and shook a couple into his hand, and Jay pointed him toward a water fountain. When Michael returned, he saw Tracy at the desk phone.

Jay was standing beside her. "Tracy, Mom and Dad haven't had time to get there," he was saying.

"I know, but I can speak to the baby-sitter. Don't worry. I'll only ask her to find the letter for me. I won't say anything." She glanced at the round clock on the wall in the waiting room.

Everyone in the room seemed to be watching the large, black rimmed clock on the wall, with its white face and black numerals. It was as though time held the same fascination for everyone. Michael stared at it as well, wondering how soon Elizabeth would come out of the coma. Even Tracy was speaking of time.

"Since it's only eight o'clock," Tracy said to Jay, "Katie probably won't be in bed yet."

Jay nodded in agreement, then walked over to sit with Michael. "I called the baby-sitter after you called us," Jay explained. "I simply told her my parents were coming to spend the night, that there had been a delay." He sighed. "She sounded like a very nice woman, but I didn't want to risk Katie over-hearing anything."

Michael nodded. "Mom will know how to handle it." He shifted in the seat and turned to Jay. "There is something else you can do for me, Jay. Do you know what happened tonight?"

Jay looked blank. "After you called, I telephoned Mom, then Tracy and I jumped in our clothes and headed across town to the hospital. I assumed...." His voice trailed off and he looked Michael squarely in the eye. "You said she was hit by a car, and that the car ran into a wall."

"Tom Robinson and another detective just left. There was another car involved, a black sports car. Tom thinks this was a hit-and-run." Michael took a deep breath and related the story he had just heard about the other driver.

Jay winced and squeezed his eyes together. Then he shook his head. "My beeper was going off all the way to the hospital. I just thought it was about another case I'm working on. I never called back. But I'll do that now. Maybe they have something."

Jay jumped from the chair and went in search of another phone.

Just then a nurse appeared in the doorway, glancing around the waiting area. "Mr. Calloway?" she called out, and her eyes met his, as though she could tell he was the person she sought.

Michael stood slowly, staring into the nurse's face, unable to speak, to even ask anything as she started toward him. He watched her approach, wanting to know, yet almost dreading to hear.

God, give me courage, he silently prayed. *I don't know what's happened to me. I've suddenly become so weak.* And then he remembered a Bible verse his mother had taught him when he was young; he had always remembered it. *"For my power is made perfect in weakness."*

"Mr. Calloway," the nurse said quickly, "your wife is still in a coma, but we're keeping her in Observation until we can get her moved up to the ICU. You can see her for just a moment, if you would like."

"Yes!" He glanced over his shoulder at Jay who was giving him a thumbs-up. He turned and followed the young nurse down a long white corridor. Some part of his brain took note of the crisp sound her uniform made as they hurried along, neither one speaking. He wanted to pummel her with questions, but he forced himself to remain silent until they reached Observation.

He focused his attention on the gleaming white floor, wondering how it was kept so clean despite heavy traffic. It occurred to him that his mind was jumping in all directions, though he attempted to remain calm.

The nurse glanced back over her shoulder. "Are you all right?" She gave him a sympathetic smile.

He nodded. "Elizabeth?"

"Her vital signs are more stable now."

He was glad she had given him that bit of good news. Otherwise, he would have panicked even more after they passed through the double doors and approached a cubicle where numerous tubes were attached to Elizabeth. He gripped the foot of the bed and stared at her. Her face was as white as the sheet covering her body. Her head was encased in a bandage, and her right arm was bandaged as well. She looked so still, so frail, he was almost afraid to touch her. And yet, he knew he must.

One nurse was studying the heart monitor, another was taking her blood pressure. He approached Elizabeth's left side cautiously as the nurse finished with the blood pressure and made a notation on the chart.

He reached over the metal rails to touch her hand, lying still at her side. Her fingers were cold, unresponsive. He squeezed them gently as he leaned over the rail and spoke to her. "Elizabeth, I'm here. I love you."

Both nurses were studying the heart monitor, but there was no change; nor did her expression indicate that she had even heard him. He could see the purple bruise on her right cheek, and there was another bandage on the side of her neck. Still, he leaned forward, pressing a kiss to her dry lips. Those lips had never been so unresponsive to him. He felt as though his heart would break if she did not come back to his world, to him and to Katie.

A doctor entered and informed everyone they were ready to move Elizabeth. One of the nurses assured Michael that he could see her every hour on the hour. He nodded, releasing Elizabeth's fingers. The slim fingers dropped back on the sheet as though he had never touched them. He backed out, his eyes never leaving the pale face he loved so much. All he could think of then was the time they had wasted with their separation, the silly disagreements that amounted to zero in light of what was happening to them now.

Michael, whose sense of direction was always on target, who could find any address in the city with just a vague description, got lost on his way back to the waiting area. He made a wrong turn down the first hallway, amazed at his stupidity. Awkwardly, he retraced his steps and found the waiting room where Jay and Tracy sat together, holding hands, staring at the floor. Just the sight of two people who cared so much gave him an added measure of strength. A minute ago he had felt as lifeless as Elizabeth looked.

They both rushed to him, their eyes wide, their lips parted. Yet neither spoke, afraid to even ask.

"She's hanging in there," he said. "They're moving her to the ICU, and I can see her every hour."

"Michael, she's going to be all right," Tracy said as she clutched his arm. "We've already called your pastor. He's alerting the church members to start round-the-clock prayers."

"And I've called Brad at Promise Keepers. The guys there are starting a prayer chain, as well."

He clutched both their hands, squeezing hard. He noticed how warm and vibrant they both felt, and again his mind slipped back to Elizabeth. He couldn't shake the image of her—so still, so pale.

"Michael, do you want us to stay with you?" Jay asked, frowning as his eyes slipped over Michael's face in an odd, searching way. Michael realized he must be acting like someone in shock. He had seen the look often in his line of work.

"I'm staying," Tracy said, turning to Jay. She looked horrified that he would even ask.

Jay turned to Tracy. "Okay. I'd like to go to headquarters to see what's being done about the hit-and-run driver. I have to do something to help, and you two are doing enough worrying for everyone."

Michael nodded. "Yeah, Jay. That would help me more than anything else you could do. I have to know what's going on; I want you to personally question everyone at the restaurant. And talk to Nick." Michael took a step closer to his brother, his mind racing ahead. "Nick may recall a customer who drives a black sports car. And the woman who saw the car. I'd like you to see her right away. You may pick up something the others have missed."

"Done," Jay nodded, then turned to Tracy. "Elizabeth wouldn't want you wearing yourself out."

"I won't, honey." She leaned up to kiss him on the cheek.

"Besides, Dad's on the way down. I called but he wouldn't hear of not coming. And I'm sure he has all the congregation praying." She turned back to Michael and spoke in a calm voice. "Michael, you and Elizabeth have lots of prayer warriors pulling for you."

Michael nodded and smiled down at his sister-in-law, realizing how much he had always liked her. She was the perfect wife for Jay, and she had fit into their family as though born to them. He leaned down and kissed her cheek. "Thanks, honey."

THREE

A police car was parked at the entrance to the Emergency Room. The man was not surprised to see it, but he knew he had to be discreet. Smoothing down the coat of his dark suit, he attempted the facade of the efficient businessman he had once been. He stopped just inside the glass doors where a guard was checking the contents of the woman's purse in front of him.

Just like security at an airport, the man thought. Trying to conceal his irritation, he removed his car keys and anything else that might set off the beeper of the security monitor.

The guard returned the purse and motioned the woman on; then his eyes swept the man, lingering on the expensive suit, and his expression changed.

Good, the man thought, *he knows I could buy and sell him if necessary.*

The guard handed back the contents of the man's pockets and motioned him into the reception area.

"Thank you," the man replied in his smooth, cultured voice.

Returning the items to his pockets, his eyes moved over the crowded waiting room. No one took especial note of him, and there was no policeman in sight. He walked to the desk and leaned over, speaking gently to the receptionist. He could have been a worried father or husband—certainly not a stalker.

"Good evening. I'm a friend of Michael Calloway's. I don't want to bother him. I just wanted to know how his wife is doing. All of his friends are concerned."

The receptionist nodded. "I understand."

Everyone knew about the terrible tragedy; there had been a special bulletin on the news. Now Atlanta's gossip machinery was buzzing.

The receptionist sighed. "This accident brought a sense of alarm to me, as well. I find myself thinking of my daughter, the same age as Mrs. Calloway." She tilted her head and looked at the man with a shy expression. "I even phoned my daughter just to be sure she was okay. I suppose that seems foolish."

"Not at all." His voice was filled with concern.

"Mrs. Calloway is in critical condition, still in a coma."

The man shook his head and heaved a deep sigh. "I don't suppose you've heard what her chances are for surviving," he asked gravely, as though the words were painful to him.

Her eyes were sad. "Not good, I'm told."

"I see," he dropped his head. "Well, thank you very much."

He turned and walked back through the glass doors to the parking area, immensely pleased with what he had learned.

Ellie had tried as gently as possible to explain to Katie what had taken place the night before. She was a very intelligent child, and it would be an insult to Katie's bright mind to try to deceive her. She already suspected that something was wrong, and she might intercept a phone call and hear the worst about her mother.

They were seated at the kitchen table, from which Grandpa Mike had abruptly excused himself, expressing a need to check on something in the backyard. Ellie knew that Mike, unlike his sons, refused to show emotion. The sight of his sad little grand-daughter as she listened to Ellie's gentle explanation of the acci-dent had been too much for him. He had already spoken with Jay twice during the night, and it was all Ellie could do to restrain him from grabbing his hunting rifle, jumping into his pickup and taking off to Atlanta to hunt down the man who had caused so much anguish.

"When can I see Mommy?" Katie asked Ellie as they sat at the kitchen table, holding hands after breakfast.

"We'll ask your daddy as soon as he comes home, darling. What we can do to help your mother most, in the meantime, is to keep on saying our prayers."

Katie's blue eyes widened as she looked at Ellie, and for a moment, Ellie saw Michael clearly in those eyes. Yet, the small features and blonde hair were like Elizabeth. She was a beautiful blend of the best of both of them. Ellie took another deep breath.

It was very hard for Ellie to remain composed. Michael and Elizabeth had already been through so much the past year. But Ellie was mother and grandmother and wife, and everyone seemed to be depending on her to keep them going. She couldn't break down now. Later, in the privacy of her room, perhaps.

"Grandma, when is Daddy coming home?" Katie pressed, refusing to let the matter rest. "When can I talk to him?"

Ellie thought about Katie's question and glanced at the kitchen clock. "I expect he or Uncle Jay will be calling us soon. I will see that you get to talk to whoever calls first. That's why I kept you out of school today."

Katie looked relieved. "Thanks, Grandma." A tiny smile hovered on her lips as she squeezed Ellie's hand. "Maybe Dad will let me come down to the hospital. I want to see Mom."

Ellie didn't know how to respond to Katie's words, and for a moment she wondered if she had made a mistake in telling her. She knew her oldest son well enough to predict that he would not want Katie seeing her mother while she was so ill.

And yet, Elizabeth was Katie's mother, and she was entitled to see her if she wished. It was so hard to advise everyone just what they should or shouldn't do. Then she reminded herself that the others were adults, more capable of coming and going as they wished than Katie was. She had to put Katie first for now.

"Tell you what," Ellie said in a bright voice. "Maybe you and I both could drive down to see your mother when it's a good time." She gave her a conspiratorial smile. "That way, we can plan things more to suit ourselves. But we can't go today. Think you can wait until tomorrow?"

Katie's smooth skin puckered in a frown between her brown brows. She seemed to be turning Ellie's words over in her mind, and Ellie prayed she would not ask to go today. "I guess that'll be okay. I'd rather go with you, anyway." She looked more comfortable with the conversation now.

"Have you talked to your friend Brooke?" Ellie asked, recalling the concerned phone call from Brooke's mother early this morning, and her generous offer to do whatever she could to help.

"No. She's already gone to school."

"Tell you what. Grandpa might drive you over to visit Brooke when she gets home from school. What if I check with her mother?"

Katie nodded. "I think she'll say yes."

Ellie smiled and nodded at Katie. "Good. Now, remember you promised to show your Grandpa where your dad's gonna put in the fishing lake."

"Right," Katie brightened. She jumped up from her chair and headed toward the back door, then hesitated. "Grandma, will you yell to us if anyone calls about Mom?"

"Sure thing, honey."

~ ~ ~ ~ ~

Katie felt better. She could trust Grandma Calloway. She had heard this morning that her other grandmother was coming from London. She hoped she wouldn't move in and try to take over. She liked the gifts her other grandmother brought her, but she was always making little suggestions about her behavior, and Katie didn't like that. And she didn't like the way she tried to boss Mom and Dad.

Well, one thing was for sure, Katie thought to herself, running down the back steps. She'd better not go bossing Mom this time. Katie had heard Mom say she wasn't going to let Grandmother Turner tell her what to do anymore. Katie liked that idea.

Michael refused to leave the hospital. He had spent the night in the waiting room, in a straight chair with his feet stretched out in another chair positioned as a foot rest. He was not going to miss an opportunity to go in and see Elizabeth. He kept hoping that if he spoke the right words, kissed her, squeezed her hand reassuringly, that her eyes would open. There had to be some way to reach her. She had to pull herself out of the coma. She had to hear him; she had to respond!

The doctors reassured him that the best neurologist in the southeast had been asked to evaluate her. All he could do now was be there for her...and pray she would come out of it.

He paced the waiting room, sick of the smells, the sights, the sounds. Yet, he was grateful for the free coffee and doughnuts, the words of encouragement from the nurses, and even the presence of those like himself who waited with strained nerves while loved ones dangled between life and death. A man had died at two this morning, and his wife and son had dissolved in tears before leaving the waiting room, clutching one another for support.

He couldn't think about that. He wouldn't let his mind entertain any negative thoughts. Tracy had stayed with him last night until Jay returned and forced her to leave at midnight.

"I don't have anything to tell you yet," Jay had reported, his voice heavy with fatigue. From the look of frustration on Jay's face, Michael knew his brother considered it a personal failure that he could not break the case immediately. "I just left the home of the woman who was seated at the window in the restaurant. So far, she's the only reliable witness we've found. And…" Jay hesitated.

"And what? Go ahead, say it," Michael prompted, trying to curb his impatience.

"I'm afraid she's not a lot of help," Jay said.

"Why not?" Michael snapped, then bit his lip. "Sorry, Jay. Just belt me one for being short with you. I know you're doing everything you can."

Jay clamped his shoulder. "It's okay, buddy. I was just as frustrated with the other detectives. I kept after them, as though they had missed something. So far, it doesn't look like they did."

"Why can't this woman help?" Michael asked.

Jay hesitated. "For starters, she wears thick glasses, and even with those, I'm not sure how adequate her vision is. All she can say for sure is that the car was dark and was, in her words, 'one of those fancy new sports models.'"

"The woman has described thousands of cars in Atlanta and the suburbs," Michael said, pounding his fist into his palm to vent his frustration.

"But this car has been wrecked," Jay pointed out. "We have

other resources to check: body shops, garages, parking lots. We know the black car has dark red paint on it. The other car involved was a maroon station wagon. So we do have something to go on. There's already a dragnet over the city, and it'll stretch to the counties by daybreak."

Michael winced, wondering how much of this he could take. He couldn't leave Elizabeth, and he couldn't go out searching for a needle in a haystack, as his secretary would say.

He shoved his hands in his pockets and rotated his neck around in a circle, trying to ease the tension there. Calling forth every ounce of determination, he tried to focus his thoughts on the facts, rather than allowing his anger to cloud his emotions.

"This woman says she saw a dark sports car?" Michael thrust his hands on his hips and faced Jay.

Jay nodded. "She isn't sure about the make or model."

Michael groaned, then pressed on. "What about her dinner companion?"

Jay shook his head. "She can't see and her husband can't hear. He had his face buried in the pasta and didn't catch on to what was happening at first. When he finally realized there had been an accident, the car was gone."

"And the hours are ticking away for other witnesses." Michael groaned the words, pacing once more. The clicking of his loafers over the white tile echoed in his ears while he tried to organize his muddled thoughts. His pacing led him to the window and he stared out at the night lights of the city he knew so well. "Memory is sharpest in the beginning. We both know that, Jay."

Jay stood beside his brother, following his line of vision out to the skyscrapers and freeways. Both men silently wondered if the hit-and-run driver was still out there somewhere. Or was he in another state by now?

Michael turned to Jay, knowing he was asking a useless question, one that had already been covered. Still, he had to ask.

"Passersby? Motorists? Pedestrians? Anyone see anything?"

Jay sighed, raking though his hair. "We'll turn up someone, Michael. Just keep the faith," Jay said bleakly, as he pulled Tracy up from the chair and put an arm around her. "Let me get her home and to bed, and I'll get back on it."

Michael reached out to hug them both. "Thanks, you two. And Jay, you get some rest yourself."

Jay merely shrugged, and Michael knew his brother would not rest until something was accomplished. He might grab a couple of hours of sleep at the most, and then he'd be back at headquarters, doing everything he could to track down the car.

A black car, one of those fancy jobs.

Michael shook his head as he slumped into the chair again and glanced at the wall clock. Another thirty minutes before he could go in and see Elizabeth.

FOUR

Everything was white. The ceiling, the walls, the world that encompassed her. Crisp. The sheets were white and crisp against her cool skin.

She turned her head on the pillow and felt it—a sensation of pressure in her brain. A flash of light, too bright for her to tolerate. She closed her eyes again, moaning softly. It seemed her head would burst, and the noise around her magnified; a noise that grated on her nerves with its constant humming sound.

Footsteps. Voices. She gritted her teeth against the assault on her senses. Then she felt a cooling numbness in her left arm, and something flowing through her veins. The voices grew louder, but mercifully the warm sleep overtook her again.

Later, she found herself staring at the white world around her. When she turned her head, drumbeats of pain shot through her. She winced and fought the pain. Did she have any control over this pain? Perhaps the best thing was not to challenge it, and so she lay completely still, trying to gather her wits.

The sounds were less irritating this time. Her eyes inched their way around her environment, checking, as her mind attempted to focus. Focus on what? She felt a slight irritation now, something other than the headache that had been her constant companion. Why the irritation? She wanted to insti- gate an awareness of where she was and why she was here. But there was an odd blank.

She told herself this was all right, she was not yet fully

awake. No need to panic. She blinked in confusion. Did she tell herself this or did another voice whisper to her? And was the voice outside or inside her brain?

She closed her eyes again and drifted back to her safe place.

There was a warmth on her arm, a soft little squeeze. His voice floated to her, gentle and soothing. It was a deep voice, male; yet there was an odd quality to the voice. The voice broke for a moment. Why had he stopped talking?

She took a deep breath, then another, and she heard the voice again. She pushed against the pressure on her eyelids. She wanted to open her eyes, respond to the voice. There was something compelling about it. She knew the voice. Yet she didn't.

Another deep long breath and she pushed harder against the force that seemed to keep her buried in sleep. It had been easy to open her eyes before. Why was it so difficult now?

A hint of daylight…then the world opened to her.

First she saw his face. He was very handsome, with deep-set eyes the color of…what? She didn't know. But she liked the eyes. A nice mixture of blue and gray. The eyes were framed by dark lashes and brown brows. A firm jaw line balanced the slim nose and long, square chin. There was a slight stubble over his face. As he captured her hand in his and lifted it to his lips, his hazel eyes suddenly filled with tears. Why? she wondered.

She tried to offer a smile of encouragement, but her lips felt numb and wobbly. It didn't matter. He was smiling for her. She could see a flash of white teeth set against nice lips that kissed her hand.

Who was he? Gently, she withdrew her hand. Something in

her upbringing—something she could not define at the moment—told her that she should not allow strangers to touch her.

He looked confused by her gesture but he was still smiling. What was he saying? She stared at him, trying to understand what he was saying.

"Welcome back." Those were his words.

From where? She was about to shake her head, indicating she didn't understand, but then the throbbing began and she winced. She could hear him calling out for someone.

When she awoke, there was another voice beside her, one that brought a strange kind of joy to her. This time her eyes opened more easily. The light around her was bright, piercing her eyes, but she was drawn toward the sweet little voice. She had to see the person who belonged to the voice.

A little girl was smiling at her. Golden blonde hair framed an oval face, and her eyes…her eyes looked familiar. She had seen those eyes recently, but where?

The man. He had the same eyes.

"Mommy, you're back!" The little girl spoke with such confidence that Elizabeth tried to smile.

"Mommy, I love you."

Then the little girl began to talk of other things—someplace that was home, things they would do together. None of this made any sense to Elizabeth, but it didn't matter. She just enjoyed being with the little girl. Her lips felt dry, even though she was aware of some kind of soothing ointment against her parched mouth. Still, she managed a wider smile. She so wanted to respond to the little girl, to say something back. All she could mutter was the thought foremost in her mind.

"You…look…so…cute." She tried to swallow but found it difficult. Strange, she thought, that she knew the shirt the little girl wore was the bright blue of a summer sky; she knew that. But she did not know the little girl's name.

Two men stood on each side of her bed, gripping the chrome rails, asking her questions. She felt the familiar irritation take over, an irritation created by noise, strange voices, unfamiliar faces. Her first inclination was to shake her head, but she remembered the pain that would come to her if she moved. She could talk, she remembered that much.

"I don't know," she answered weakly. And that was true. She knew nothing. Her mind was a total blank. She had no idea of…many things. Who she was, or how the people hovering about the room with expressions of concern on their faces fit into her life. Was this a bad dream? Was she going to wake up and find that everything made sense? She hoped so. Otherwise, she wished they would all go away.

Carefully, her eyes scanned the sea of faces, seeking the cute little girl. But she was not among them. She closed her eyes again. It didn't really matter who the others were.

Millicent Turner paced the waiting room adjacent to the ICU, her jeweled hands gripped tightly in frustration and fear. Never in her life had she been through anything like this.

Well, there had been one other time but she tried not to think of that day when two somber-faced men stood at her front door and delivered the words, each one a blow to her heart. Her husband's plane had been shot down over Vietnam. While his body had not been found, the wreckage of the plane gave little hope.

The memory faded as Franklin, her second husband,

approached her with a Styrofoam cup of steaming coffee. She stared at the coffee. It looked as though it had been well cooked since breakfast.

"You know my stomach won't tolerate that stuff," she snapped at him. He had tried to force food on her, food she couldn't eat, drinks that scalded her tongue. The bad food and horrible coffee were accompanied by meaningless consolations. She thought she loved Franklin but at times, like now, she found him bothersome and downright irritating.

He retreated from her, placing the ugly-looking black coffee on a table. Then he sank into a chair and proceeded to sip his own coffee.

At the sound of footsteps, she whirled to face Michael.

"Is there any news?"

He shook his head.

She plunged in then, her tone intolerant of those who did not jump to please, fetch, or fix. "She doesn't recognize me, Michael. That's quite obvious. What do the doctors say? And I must tell you, I think we should fly her to a better hospital."

A weary-looking Michael put up a hand, halting her tumbling words. "We have a capable team of doctors here who do not want her moved. This is a very delicate situation, Millicent. Furthermore, Emory is a fine hospital, and I'm not sure I would take her someplace else. The best neurosurgeon—"

"What about Mayo?" she cut him off. "Or Houston? We can charter a plane."

Michael's eyes ran over her face. She looked nothing like Elizabeth except for the brown eyes. Elizabeth had told him she was like her father in every way.

He turned away, raking a hand through his tousled hair. As usual, Millicent had not heard a word he had spoken. He wanted to shout her down, but she was Elizabeth's mother. Unlike

Ellie, who remained in the background, concerned with Katie, Millicent's only concern was "fixing" Elizabeth, and it was not going to be that easy.

"We're scheduled to meet with the neurologist in…" he checked his watch, "fifteen minutes. I hope to get some answers from him." He hesitated, then continued in a firm voice. "We will listen quietly to everything he tells us, then make our evaluations later." He squared his shoulders and looked directly into her brown eyes. "I have no intention of alienating the man who will prove most helpful to Elizabeth if we allow him to do his job. He's one of the best in the southeast and we must trust him for now."

Millicent straightened her tall frame in the white linen suit. Studying her, Michael knew her aversion to wrinkles; fortunately, she was unaware that her clothes did not display perfection. The short brown hair was lacquered in place; the application of her makeup was adequate, except for the tiny smear of mascara below her left eye, the aftermath of her tears. He noticed she kept glancing at him out of the corner of her eye. He wondered what she was thinking; on the other hand, he didn't really care. Elizabeth was foremost in his mind; she was the center of his concern.

Something about the way Michael spoke to her had silenced Millicent. She had never thought Michael equal to Elizabeth and had tried to pick fights with him on many occasions. This time, with her daughter's life on the line, she chose to hold her tongue and wait, although patience was not her virtue. She turned to Franklin. He was the epitome of patience, but at times this annoyed her. She couldn't fight with him, either. With a sigh of resignation, she took her seat beside him, ignoring the coffee, as they sat waiting for the doctor to make his appearance.

Her eyes roamed the waiting room, unimpressed with the decor, although she supposed some found it soothing, even nice. She had always wanted the best for Elizabeth, and she wanted that now. But she was being forced to quiet down, give this doctor the benefit of a doubt. What else could she do at this point? It would be unwise to provoke a fight she couldn't win.

Her eyes felt gritty from lack of sleep, but she turned again to Michael, studying him for a long, thoughtful moment.

He had matured, changed. He did not quietly submit as he had done in the past. This time he…well, he challenged her. She was not sure if she resented this or admired it. She had been against the idea of moving Elizabeth from the ICU to a private room, although Michael assured her she was still being monitored in every way. The fact was, she was no longer in critical condition, and for this, they should be grateful and happy.

Drawing a deep breath, Millicent lowered her eyes to her hands, clenched in her lap. The new stone Franklin had bought for her on their anniversary captured her attention. She tilted her right hand slightly, admiring the richness of the ruby in its platinum setting.

Suddenly her thoughts swung to Katie, whom she loved. Someday she would give the ring to Katie. The faint creases in her high forehead deepened with concern. Katie was not as affectionate as she had expected. Of course Ellie Calloway was to blame, Ellie and her uncouth husband. They were always trying to monopolize Katie, absorb all of her attention. It didn't matter. In time, she would fix that too. There was nothing money couldn't buy, and she would shower Katie with love in the form of gifts when the time was right. They would fly to Paris together, see the museums, catch a few fashion shows. Millicent could teach Katie a lot about fashion.

She leaned back in the chair, relaxing a bit. For the first time in the last horrid twenty-four hours, she felt better. Her thoughts drifted on to imaginary shopping trips with Katie. She would enjoy helping her select the perfect outfits with matching handbags and shoes. And perfect little jewelry. That thought lifted her spirits even more. Yes, their best days were ahead, so she would let the Calloways monopolize her only grandchild for now.

She took a deep breath and turned to Franklin. "I *would* like some herbal tea, but please not so hot that it scalds my mouth, as it did yesterday."

"Of course." He jumped to his feet, anxious to accommodate.

She watched him go. He was a small man, shorter than she, but she respected his business acumen, his culture, his manners. And she liked to spend his money.

Her thoughts brightened as they waited for the neurosurgeon. At least she and Michael would be alone to speak with the doctor. The other in-laws had left, taking Katie back to Oak Shadows where Michael seemed to want to keep her. He made an argument for keeping Katie busy with her normal routine, easing the trauma of what had happened to her mother. Millicent supposed that made sense. She just didn't want his country parents instilling nonsense in Katie's head. In her opinion, they were religious fanatics.

Her mother had been religious, she remembered, and she herself had been, well, more faith oriented when she was growing up at Oak Shadows. But something happened to her faith when her beloved husband's plane was shot down and she was left widowed with a child to raise in the country. Millicent bored easily, and she had quickly tired of long, dull days at Oak Shadows. Elizabeth seemed to thoroughly enjoy her life there. Millicent had visions of moving out as quickly as possible, move into the city, to someplace exciting. But she wasn't able to do that until later, not with Elizabeth to raise. Millicent had begun to resent the fact that her mother obviously managed Elizabeth better than she. And worse, Elizabeth seemed to prefer being with her grandmother more than her own mother.

Suddenly, a man dressed in a white coat over white shirt, conservative tie, and dark slacks appeared. Michael was coming to his feet, glancing at Millicent.

"We can meet in the conference room down the hall," the doctor said to Michael.

Millicent frowned at the doctor. She doubted he was a day over forty. Again, she felt suspicion and the need to argue rising within her, but she held her tongue. She would listen to what the man had to say. Then, if she didn't agree, she would insist that Elizabeth be taken elsewhere.

Michael could hear the clipping of Millicent's spike heels trailing behind, and again he thought how different this woman was from Elizabeth. Elizabeth would be dressed in practical clothing, sensible shoes. This was not a social gathering, it was a hospital where life over death was the main concern. No one here was trying to make a fashion statement, as Elizabeth would say; frankly, nobody seemed to care what anyone wore.

Dr. Cope led them into a small yet comfortable room with a conference table and cushioned chairs. He sat down at the head of the table and opened Elizabeth's file.

"Mrs. Calloway's vital signs are stable," he said, looking

through the papers. "The last scan indicated no permanent damage to her brain, and the medication is improving her headaches. Hopefully the amnesia will clear up in a few days."

"Hopefully?" Millicent blurted.

"Head injuries are difficult to analyze," he continued smoothly, looking down the table to Millicent. "The dizziness she first experienced has passed, or at least she's learned to move her head slowly to prevent it. There's been no more nausea, although she claims to be experiencing insomnia." He looked back at the file. "I'm prescribing a mild sedative to help her rest."

Michael listened intently, grateful that Elizabeth was doing so well. Miraculously, there were no broken bones, just severe bruises. Her head had hit the concrete of the parking lot, initiating the brain concussion. He realized again how fortunate they were that Elizabeth had survived.

"And so," the doctor said, "the only problem we're dealing with is the amnesia. I could use long medical terms about this, but I think you would prefer the basics. In simple terms, I believe the amnesia has blocked out all but some bits and pieces of childhood. When I question her, she seems to be more responsive to her early years. You simply have to start there and build your way up to the present with her."

He closed the file. "Every patient is different. I can give no guarantees, but I would expect her memory to clear fairly soon. She may seem restless, sensitive to noise, even paranoid at times, but these are usual side effects." He was thoughtful for a moment, then he looked at Michael.

"I agree with you that she is more likely to respond to familiar surroundings. In my experience, prolonging a patient's stay in the hospital does not improve memory, particularly if that person is healthy in every other way."

"You're certain she's healthy?" Millicent challenged. "She looks so pale, so...*sick.*"

"That's a result of the trauma. I think fresh air, sunshine, and the companionship of her loved ones is what she needs most." A faint smile played over his mouth as Dr. Cope looked into Michael's eyes. He seemed to understand the deep love Michael felt for Elizabeth.

"I see no reason why she can't go home tomorrow." His eyes swept Michael. "You're obviously a caring and sensitive man. But be patient with her." His eyes strayed to Millicent, silently making a point. "I know it's difficult when your loved one doesn't seem to know you."

Michael took a deep breath. "I can handle that."

"Also..." The doctor was trying to make another point. "I advise families not to aggravate the patient's anxiety by referring to the accident unless necessary." He paused, frowning a bit. "I understand the police need to question her further, but this seems to make her more nervous because she can't answer their questions. If there is some way..."

"I can handle that too," Michael cut in. "I'll be very protective of her. Getting her out of the city, back to the home where she was raised will give us more privacy."

The doctor stood and smiled at Michael and Millicent. "You're very fortunate that amnesia is her only problem, although I realize it's a frustrating one."

"We're just glad she's alive," Michael responded, shaking the doctor's hand.

The man was parked in the shadows in a remote section of the visitors lot. He had circled the entire hospital parking area until he located the car Michael Calloway had been driving. Then he had patiently waited for an older couple to back their car out so he could grab a space at a comfortable distance from Michael; still he wanted to be close enough to note the departure of the detective.

A few discreet phone calls had garnered the information he needed. Brain concussion resulting in amnesia. But would the amnesia clear when she saw him?

The man studied the clock on his dash. Visiting hours would be over in another ten minutes. If he waited any longer, he might be unable to get inside the hospital and find his way to Elizabeth's room.

He mentally reviewed the latest update on her condition. She had been moved out of Intensive Care to a private room. He had memorized the room number, and he had already checked out the location. He knew exactly where to find her.

What to do? He didn't want to chance running into Michael, who unlike his amnesiac wife, would know him immediately from their past association with a fund-raiser last month. He might even remember the Jaguar he had owned. He sighed with relief. That car had been sold to an underworld car dealer and was now stashed in a body shop in Chicago. It would never be found.

He squinted through the darkness, over the parked cars to the brightly lit front doors of the hospital. The evening crowd was filing out, and he did not want to be denied entry to the patient's room after visiting hours. He had to know one, all-important question, and this was his only chance to get an answer.

Deciding on the least dangerous of his alternatives, he got out of his car, pushing the automatic lock on the doors. He would merely turn his head and walk in another direction if he saw Calloway coming. Once inside the hospital, he could take a back corridor up to the fifth floor. He had devised a plan.

He walked briskly through the main doors. He was dressed casually this evening—a white knit shirt, khakis, and loafers. He usually presented the image of a sleek, first-rate business-man. Tonight, he looked more like a college professor, he decided, glimpsing his image in the glass windows of the gift shop.

His breath caught as he recognized the tall, lean figure of Michael Calloway stepping off the elevator. The man whirled back into the gift shop, watching Michael as he crossed the lobby, his hands shoved in his pockets, his head down. Just as the man was about to turn, he saw Michael cast a quick glance over the scattering crowd, as though searching for someone. A relative? Or was he already on the lookout for the man driving a black sports car, a man with no description?

The man breathed a deep sigh of relief as Michael strolled out of the hospital. Then, whirling on his heel, he made a dash for the bank of elevators, catching one door just before it closed.

"Almost got you," a woman said with a smile.

"Yes, it did." He gave her a pleasant nod as he stepped on the elevator, his eyes sweeping over her quickly.

She was middle-aged, dressed in tan slacks and a white sweater. In her arms, she carried a pillow and a quilt. She was spending the night here, he made a mental note as he punched the button for the fourth floor. His plan was to exit there, then climb the stairs to the north end of the fifth floor where Elizabeth's room was located.

The halls were emptying of people, some saying last good-byes until the next day. Unobtrusively, he hurried on, turning his head sideways to study a wall clock as he passed the nurses' station. On to the Exit sign at the end of the hall he went, his loafers clicking lightly over the tiled corridor.

He knew how he looked to those who darted a quizzical glance: clean cut and neat, wearing clothes that were expensively understated. No doubt he appeared to be a family man, a concerned father or husband.

Gripping the metal hand rail, he moved quickly up the stairs, wondering about his next plan. Everything depended on who was around her room, watching.

He entered the corridor of the fifth floor, gently closing the door behind him. A medicine cart was parked before the nearest room; must be time for patients to get their bedtime dosage of medications.

Sidestepping the cart, he ambled up the corridor. One man sat in a chair in the hallway, reading a newspaper. *He was a detective.* He had the look of a detective, and he had no other reason to be here, if he were not.

Turning into a small waiting room, the man hurried to the telephone booth and stepped inside, closing the door. There were only two people in the waiting room, he noted, a man and woman who looked exhausted. They hardly noticed him.

His hands were beginning to shake, and he cursed his weakness. This had to be done right, he told himself, reaching into his shirt pocket for the number of the nurses' station nearby. Inserting a quarter, he dialed the number. After several rings, a pleasant voice came on.

"Fifth floor nurses' station, this is Cindy."

He cleared his throat. "Hi, Cindy, this is Lieutenant Wilkens. I need to speak to my man down the hall near Mrs. Calloway's room."

"Just a minute," she answered swiftly.

Immediately, he hung up the phone, stepped out of the telephone booth and ventured to the door. The nurse had approached the detective and was whispering to him. He came to his feet, folding the newspaper under his arm as his eyes swept the hall, right and left.

The man held his position in the door of the waiting room, until the detective turned his back and started toward the telephone at the nurses' station, located just around the corner.

There was no time to lose, not a second! The man walked quickly to Elizabeth Calloway's room and poked his head around the door.

She lay very still against the white sheets. She was elevated in the hospital bed, which somehow made her appear even more frail. She stared blankly at the mounted television screen until he cleared his throat.

"Excuse me, I was looking for Mrs. Dillard's room."

She turned her head and looked directly into his eyes. He held his breath, momentarily paralyzed with fear. Then his mind registered the blank expression in her brown eyes.

"Who?" she asked weakly.

He gave her a warm smile. "Sorry, wrong room."

Moving quickly back into the hall, he slowed his pace and strolled casually toward the stairs, never looking back. He had no idea if the detective was making his way back to his chair, or was already searching the waiting room. He could not afford to glance over his shoulder. Gently, he opened the door and hurried down the stairs, half expecting the door to be yanked open behind him. But there was only the sound of his loafers echoing in the hollow stairwell. He took the stairs all the way down to the first floor, never slowing up, his heart pounding rapidly by the time he reached the bottom.

Then he was out the front door and back into the shadows of the parking area, breathing a slow deep sigh of relief. Elizabeth Calloway had not recognized him.

Elizabeth's eyes lingered on the door for a few seconds, wondering about the little man who was looking for someone. She was looking for someone too. Elizabeth Calloway.

The man whom she knew as Frank stuck his head in the door, looking anxious. "Are you all right?"

"Fine," she responded weakly, thinking how untrue that was as he nodded again then disappeared.

My mind is one giant blank space, but I'm just fine, she thought, amazed that she could utter the word. Did she know what the word meant? Of course she did. She knew what words meant, she just didn't know the people who spoke them.

Elizabeth sighed, recalling the gentle questions her husband had asked. He tried not to look disappointed when she had no answers to his questions, but even if his face was strange to her, somehow human nature was not. She could read his body language and noted the slump of defeat in his shoulders. She knew so little: that she was in the hospital as the result of a car wreck, that she was married to the man who stayed by her side and rarely left the room, and that the beautiful little girl was her daughter; but these were facts her brain merely assembled from what she was told. She knew very little about herself: her present height, the food she liked, other than ice cream, the music she enjoyed, the things in life that brought her pleasure.

She found escape in sleep. When she closed her eyes, she could shut out the concerned faces with their endless questions, but only sleep would shut out the helplessness and frustration.

Her nurse for the evening shift entered her room, carrying her nightly medication. Elizabeth forced a weak smile and gratefully accepted the sedative. Maybe when she awoke the next day, she would remember who she was.

~ ~ ~ ~ ~

When morning came, her mind was still a blank, and Elizabeth fought back tears of disappointment. Dutifully, she followed the instructions of the older nurse as she led her into the shower. The warm spray of the water on her thin body felt good to Elizabeth. She enjoyed showers, she told herself, clinging to that one awareness. Afterwards, she was exhausted, and she collapsed gratefully into her freshly changed bed.

"Today is the big day," a young blonde nurse said as she waltzed into the room sometime later. Above a cotton jacket, short-sleeved, with a small floral pattern, blue eyes twinkled. A wide smile curved over even, white teeth. How old was this woman? Elizabeth wondered. And how did one judge?

And how old am I? she wondered, feeling that sense of panic again.

"You're going home," the young nurse reminded her, hands on hips, looking at her with that happy smile that Elizabeth found…well, irritating.

The nurse wheeled a tan metal tray before her and yanked open a drawer.

"Your makeup case is in here."

She flipped back the top of the tray and Elizabeth faced herself. It was not the first time she had looked into the mirror, and yet her expression never seemed to change.

Staring into the mirror, she met a pair of confused, brown eyes. The eyes were set into deep hollows, with dark lashes and arched brown brows. The eyes felt odd, as though she wanted to close them often. The face was thin, the cheeks slightly sunken above a square jawline. Her mouth was well-formed yet the lips were quite pale. Did she normally wear makeup and lipstick?

The hair that framed her face was not blonde, not brown,

but somewhere in between. In the morning light, it was the color of the honey she had spread on her toast at breakfast.

She was conscious of a slight weight in her hand, and she looked down to the cosmetic bag the nurse had given her. The nurse unzipped it, attempting to be helpful, Elizabeth supposed.

"Here you go." The nurse gave her the wide, dimpled smile again, but this time Elizabeth did not return it. She turned her attention to the cosmetic bag, searching for a clue to her personality.

Carefully, she examined the contents inside with childlike curiosity. A one-ounce bottle of moisturizing matte makeup—"natural beige," the bottom of the bottle read. A small pot of lip gloss—"deep wine." A small gold compact with pressed powder, another compact with a brush and russet powder.

"This will add a bit of color to your cheeks," the nurse explained patiently, pointing to the russet powder.

Elizabeth nodded, picking up a slim wand of mascara—"black velvet." At the bottom of the makeup kit there was an eyebrow pencil, natural brown, with a sharp point. Those were the sole contents of the makeup bag, and Elizabeth could not remember ever using any of these things.

"You have to get ready now," the nurse urged politely. "Your husband left a pretty pantsuit for you. Shall I help you with your hair?"

Not responding to the question, Elizabeth lifted a hand to her head. The hair felt silky after a dry shampoo yesterday.

"We have to be careful with your head," the nurse warned. "How is the headache?"

"Always there," Elizabeth responded honestly as she zipped up the bag. "I don't want to wear makeup today," she said, wishing she didn't sound so defiant.

A brown brow hiked. "Okay, suit yourself. Shall I get your clothes?"

Elizabeth nodded. She couldn't leave the hospital in the blue silk pajamas the intrusive woman—her mother—had left for her. With a sigh of resignation, she began the business of dressing.

Later, she sat in the chair, watching indifferently as nurses swept in and out of the room. She tried to concentrate but her thoughts were muddled.

Home. She was going home. But where was home? Elizabeth thought of flowers in a garden, a woman with a sun hat shielding her smooth fair skin, and wrinkles that crinkled the kind brown eyes. The memory of that woman made her feel good. But…She sighed.

That was not the woman, her mother, who darted around, pulling perfumes and powders from fancy little gift bags.

Strange, she thought, staring into space. The knowledge that the woman was her mother had come to her, but there had been no comfort in that knowledge.

She pressed her head gently against the back of the chair and thought back to the scene here in her room two—or was it three?—days ago. All the days seemed to melt and flow into one another.

"These are for you, darling," the woman had said as she stood beside the hospital bed. "I made a quick trip to Saks to get the perfume you always loved. I wasn't certain you had any at home."

The woman's tone changed slightly as she looked at the man on the opposite side of the bed, the man named Michael who held Elizabeth's hand and had told her he was her husband.

Elizabeth recalled the scene as one watching a play. Or she supposed that's how it seemed; she thought she had attended plays.

She recalled studying the woman carefully before answering.

The woman was middle-aged, with light brown hair and brown eyes. The man with her, who seemed to always hover in the background, was a complete stranger. Then a memory had stirred. She reached out her hand, and the woman was delighted.

"Oh, darling, you do remember me, don't you?" the woman asked, flinging a triumphant glance at Michael.

"Yes," Elizabeth spoke quietly, "I think I do."

The woman was absolutely beaming now. "Oh Franklin, isn't this wonderful? She remembers me when—"

She had broken off her careless flow of speech. At least she had the grace not to say what was obvious to all. *She remembers me when she doesn't remember Michael or Katie....*

Recalling the incident, Elizabeth heaved a weary sigh. In her heart, she knew the woman was her mother, but there was no joy with that knowledge. Why not? There was no answer to that either.

Fighting the frustration that always accompanied the blank spaces, she turned her attention to the clothes her husband had brought for her to wear today. The pantsuit was white, size eight, well made. She ran her fingers over the smooth linen covering her thigh. She must have weighed quite a bit more before this, for now the pants and cropped top with black buttons were loose about her body. During her morning shower, Elizabeth had studied her slim body and decided her figure was all right; she didn't see any major flaws. The nurse had helped her style her hair in smooth deep waves that ended just above her shoulders. The final effect, she supposed, was pleasing. At least, the nurse thought she looked pretty. But she didn't know if she was pretty or not; there was still so much she didn't know.

Suddenly, the woman—her mother—and her mother's companion burst into the room.

"Darling," her mother said, squeezing her hand, "we have a suite at the Hilton. Would you like to go there with Franklin and me?" She clutched the shy man's arm, yanking him forward. "That way we'd be close to the hospital and—"

"Millicent," Michael spoke up from the doorway, "you remember the doctor agreed that Elizabeth should return to Oak Shadows because—"

"Oak Shadows," Elizabeth interrupted, suddenly feeling wistful. "That's where the garden is."

Michael whirled to her, looking both surprised and pleased. "Yes, you have a lovely flower garden there. Katie and the garden have been missing you."

She suddenly felt better as she thought about the garden.

"Yes," she looked from Michael to her mother, "that's where I want to go." She tried to smile. She wanted to go back to the garden and to Oak Shadows. That name meant something to her. Yes, she felt certain that was home.

"I still feel you should rent a nice place near the hospital for the next few weeks. She might—"

"She's going to be fine," Michael had assured her. "And we're going home." There was a final note to his voice, as though the conversation had ended.

As Elizabeth looked from her mother and the man named Franklin back to Michael, she tried desperately to piece her life together. There was a lot she didn't know, yet one thing was obvious. These two did not get along, did not even like one another. Her memory began to sharpen as she listened to her mother's persistent whine. Elizabeth thought back to her childhood. She did not feel the kind of warm joy for her mother that she felt for the woman in the garden. Maybe the woman in the garden would be waiting for her when she got home.

She pressed her slim hands against the arm rest and tried to stand. Michael came forward to help her, for her legs were shaky. She wondered when she would stop feeling so weak.

Her eyes trailed over the room that had been her home for…however long. She was glad to be leaving.

FIVE

Michael was taking great satisfaction in the sequence of events. Elizabeth had overcome her mother's objections by expressing a wish to go to Oak Shadows. This was reassuring to Michael. It was draining to constantly take a stand against Millicent all by himself.

Now, as they rode home in silence, Elizabeth kept staring out the window at the passing scenery, fascinated.

He cleared his throat as they wound through the quiet town of Springville, heading to Oak Shadows.

"Do you remember the history connected to Oak Shadows?" he asked gently.

She turned her head and looked at him very much like Katie would have, with a kind of childlike wonder. "I think…it has something to do with my ancestors. What is it?"

Michael smiled, stretching his arm across the steering wheel, as the cooling ripple of the air conditioner offset the warm day. "You are an Irish descendant. The man who homesteaded Oak Shadows was named Jack O'Malley. He wanted to be a cotton farmer, and apparently he was a very successful one. He was good at his work. He married a local woman and they built Oak Shadows, which was completed a year before the Civil War. His daughter was your great-great-grandmother and is buried in the family cemetery on the grounds."

Elizabeth smiled faintly. "This sounds like a story I've heard before. Is that a good sign?"

He reached over to clasp her hands, folded demurely in her lap. "It's a very good sign."

"What about Mother?" she said. She looked curiously at

Michael. "I sense a tension between us, and between her and everyone except that little man who caters to her."

"Franklin," Michael nodded. "Well, I'd rather stay away from any discussion of your mother just now."

"I think I understand. Oddly, I do remember her, and I feel an affection for her, but—"

"She and your father were living in Marietta when you were born," Michael interrupted smoothly, trying to avoid unpleasant subjects. "You were very young when your father joined the army in the Vietnam War." He stopped there, wondering if she remembered that he was killed in Vietnam.

Her smooth brow puckered in a frown. "Something happened to him," she said vaguely.

Michael was always sorry about Elizabeth's loss; she had told him she was much more like her father, and he had no doubt of that. "Yes, he was killed in Vietnam."

She took a deep breath and turned her brown eyes back to the road. "I don't have much memory of those years...they're muddled, confused. I do remember having a playmate named...Allison. That must have been in Marietta. She and her family lived in a duplex next to ours. We had tea parties."

Her brown eyes had taken on a slight glow. Michael could see she was pleased by that memory, or perhaps she was pleased that she could remember the tea parties at all.

"Very good," he said, winking at her.

"The next thing I remember is living at a place with lots of trees and grass, a big house, and a beautiful flower garden."

"Right. And here we are."

As Michael turned up the lane to Oak Shadows, he felt his chest swell with pride. He and Elizabeth had worked long, tedious hours in the evenings and on weekends, building this into a home they could both love. Michael had spent an inordinate amount of time on the grounds, clearing away all the overgrown vines and tall weeds, planting new grass, restoring the grounds to their natural beauty. Jay and Dad had pitched in to help two weekends; otherwise, he could never have accomplished so much on his own.

He now reaped the benefits of everyone's labor as he and Elizabeth drove home. He understood her deep affection for Oak Shadows, for now he shared that feeling. He glanced at her, noting her expression as she looked at the white picket fence they had just erected only weeks before. She had always wanted a white picket fence, and this had been Michael's birthday present to her. The shrubs were well pruned; the magnolia tree spread out its massive branches to provide deep shade.

"It's very pretty," she said slowly, glancing from the grounds to Michael, "and it seems familiar to me."

Elizabeth knew Michael expected her to respond, and she was trying. In truth, however, what she recalled was something in the recesses of her brain. A memory of this place being viewed in a blur, as though she were running.

"I remember...running across this lawn. I remember that, Michael," she said, suddenly feeling hopeful.

Michael gently squeezed her hand. She supposed he was trying to reassure her.

"Oh Elizabeth, it's all going to come back. I'm sure of that."

She hoped he was right. She still felt odd about his touching her, and when she looked at him, she saw a very kind man...but sadly, he was still a stranger to her. She couldn't bear to say that to him, for she sensed that he loved her very much. Actually, he had told her that over and over, but she could not bring herself to respond in kind. How could you say that to someone you didn't even know?

He was stopping the car before the house, and her breath caught in her throat.

The house was a grand, white brick structure. Thick columns rose past the second story to the roof, from which jutted smaller windows. The same pattern was repeated on the side verandah. Black shutters graced the long windows with matching black wrought-iron furniture on the front porch. On the upper verandah lush green ferns hung in baskets. It was all very lovely. But for some reason this place did not feel quite right.

She turned and looked at the man behind the wheel. He looked so hopeful, and she knew he was waiting for her to say something. She couldn't bear to disappoint him. In a way the house and grounds were familiar, yet in another way it was not the home she remembered.

"The house…" She shook her head. "It isn't quite the house I remember. I…I think maybe it's prettier."

Michael smiled. "Darling, your memory is restoring itself the same way we stacked Katie's building blocks when she was little."

She stared at him, puzzled by that explanation.

"Remember how we'd start with the foundation and build upward to make a toy for her? You're rediscovering your childhood; it's only a matter of time until the foundation reaches upward to me and to Katie. What you're remembering now is the way the house looked when you were that child running across the lawn." He paused, glancing back at the house. "We had to brace the columns, repaint the exterior, add new shutters, and patch the roof."

She pushed against the blank wall in her mind. This was not quite the house she remembered, and for some odd reason she was disappointed. But she wanted to hide that emotion, so she took a deep breath and looked back at Michael.

She tried to find the right words for a response. "That sounds like a lot of work. Was it?"

"Yes, it was a lot of work." He was nodding slowly, as though recalling all they had done. "Yet, I enjoyed the satisfaction we felt each time we completed a job, and so did you. Oh Elizabeth, everything was working out so well for us when—"

She turned and looked at him. What was he thinking? she wondered.

Michael pressed his lips together firmly and got out of the car. As he approached the passenger's side, he watched Elizabeth carefully. He smiled at the eagerness in her eyes. Surely if she could remember her early childhood the rest would come back to her in time.

The front door banged and Elizabeth jumped. Michael realized she was feeling on edge, but he resisted the impulse to slow Katie down.

Katie was wearing her favorite jeans and yellow T-shirt. Her blonde hair bounced around her happy face as she ran to greet them.

Elizabeth stared at her. "She's such a cute little girl, isn't she? What's her name, again?"

That question stunned Michael, although he should have adjusted to this by now.

"That's Katie, our daughter," he said quietly.

Elizabeth turned back to him, her eyes filling with tears. "And I can't remember her. How terrible!"

"Come on, put on a good face," he said under his breath. "She's so happy to have you back home. Be brave."

"Yes, I'll try."

Michael swallowed hard, trying to conceal the sadness and frustration warring within him. How could she not remember Katie, her own daughter? It had been difficult enough to deal with the fact that she regarded him as a stranger. He wanted so badly to hold her in his arms, to kiss her and tell her how much he loved her; but each time he made the slightest attempt at intimacy, she had shied away, her brown eyes signaling caution. He had to give her time, he reminded himself. It would all come back in time.

As Katie reached them, he swooped her up in a bear hug, and whispered to her to be easy with her mother, that she was still sick. "We have to be patient," he reminded her softly.

Katie nodded. She seemed to understand. And he knew he had his mother to thank. He must remember to express his appreciation to his parents, who had rushed here from Moonglow to help out in any and every way possible. Thank God, Millicent had decided to go shopping today. They would be free of her for a little while. Again, Michael attempted to curb any unkind thoughts about his mother-in-law.

"Hi, Mom," Katie said in her most ladylike voice as she stood with her hands clutched at her sides, looking up at her mother with love-filled eyes.

"Hi, there. You're so pretty," Elizabeth said, hesitating for a moment. And then she reached out to Katie, hugging her lightly. Katie's little arms flew around her mother's waist, and Michael grinned, thinking little Katie seemed more robust than her mother.

"Take it easy, Hon," Michael touched his daughter's shoulder.

"Oh, I forgot," Katie said, stepping back and beaming up at her mother. "You have to get your strength back."

~ ~ ~ ~ ~

Elizabeth smiled down at her, wondering how she knew that. What a smart little girl she was, so perceptive, so adorable.

The front door opened and closed and Elizabeth looked up, expecting to see her mother. Instead, a tall, middle-aged woman with a friendly smile was walking down the steps to greet her. She had no idea who the woman was, and again that sense of panic began to build within her. When was the confusion going to clear? And how was she supposed to act toward people until she knew who these various people were?

Her hands were trembling slightly as the woman touched them.

"Hello, Elizabeth. You must be anxious to get to your room and rest. I've turned the covers down for you, and Michael can get your things from the car."

Ellie's eyes lingered on Elizabeth for only a fraction, aware that her daughter-in-law did not recognize her. However, she was pleased to see that her brown eyes glowed in her pale face when she looked at the house. With Katie trailing after her, Elizabeth began to walk toward the front steps. Ellie turned to Michael, watching him with sympathy as he unloaded the car. She couldn't begin to imagine the agony he must be feeling. She looked again at Elizabeth and Katie. Elizabeth had stopped to admire the red petunias bordering the walk.

"This really feels like home," she said, smiling down at Katie.

Ellie felt her throat tighten, and she grabbed a breath and squared her shoulders. "I've cooked plenty of food to hold all of you for a few days, Michael. Dad and I are going back to Moonglow to give you some privacy."

Michael set down Elizabeth's suitcase as they reached the porch and turned to envelop his mother in his arms. She hugged him back, thinking how much he must need someone to comfort him, to help bear the burdens.

"I can't thank you enough for all you've done."

"That's what family is all about, darling." She stepped back from him and looked into his troubled eyes. "It's going to be fine, honey. Just give yourselves time."

He nodded, taking a deep breath. "Where's Dad?"

"Puttering around the backyard. You know how he hates scenes. I'm afraid he's still of the old school when it comes to showing his emotions, so let's just let him be macho. I guess he's too old to change."

In the background Katie was chattering to Elizabeth as they mounted the porch steps together, arm in arm. Ellie used the opportunity to lower her voice. "Any news?"

Michael shook his head quickly.

"Your brother is working night and day," she whispered under her breath.

Michael nodded. "I know. He and Tracy have been fantastic. Before you leave, I want to find Dad and say hello."

Ellie nodded. "When your dad heard that Elizabeth probably wouldn't recognize him at first, he thought it would be best if we came back later."

Michael was listening to his mother, nodding in agreement, but his concentration was focused on Elizabeth and Katie. They had taken a seat in the porch chairs. Looking more relaxed, Elizabeth was gazing out across the lawns, and for once she looked happy.

"I like to sit here, don't you?" she said as she looked down at Katie.

"Sure, Mom. We sit here a lot."

She reached down and clutched Katie's hand. "You are such a precious child."

Katie beamed up at her mother, pleased by the compliment, but Ellie and Michael exchanged a sad glance.

Michael sighed. "I'll go around back and speak to Dad."

Carrying her suitcase, he climbed the steps to the porch and looked at Elizabeth, then Katie.

"Katie, your mom may need to rest for a little bit," he said. When Katie frowned at the idea, he reached out to pat her shoulder. "Why don't you show your mother the flowers Jay and Tracy sent?" he suggested with a wink.

"Okay." She glanced curiously at her mother.

As they entered the house, Michael watched Elizabeth carefully. She had stopped in the hallway and was frowning at the soft pink walls she had painted herself. Michael hadn't been sure about the idea of pink when she first mentioned it, but when it was done he liked the contrast to the white trim on the door facings and window frames.

Elizabeth's eyes dropped to the floor, to the freshly sanded wood, overlaid with an Oriental runner. She and the decorator had carefully chosen all the rugs on their trips into Atlanta.

"This is all wrong," she said, whirling back to Michael. "This isn't Grandmother's home." Her eyes were filling with tears. She looked like a little girl who had suddenly realized she had entered the wrong house. She made a half circle, staring at the walls. "The walls were white."

Katie gasped loudly, turning to her father with a look of panic. Michael, too, was feeling a bit panicky, but he tried to keep his voice calm as he spoke. Looking from his wide-eyed daughter to his tearful wife, he knew he had to be the anchor here.

"Elizabeth, the walls were white but when we redecorated, you wanted pink."

He reached for her hand, and felt her fingers stiffen. "Listen to me," he said gently. "This is still your grandmother's house, but the white walls were dingy and needed painting. Your memory is coming back slowly. Soon you'll recall choosing this color. As a matter of fact, you were very picky about getting this shade of pink. You copied the color from a book of antebellum homes that had been redone."

"And you told me not to touch anything," Katie spoke up, trying to be helpful, yet she had taken a couple of steps back from her mother, as though frightened by what she was witnessing.

Michael wanted to protect his daughter, his wife, himself. But how?

He set down the suitcase and followed Elizabeth's gaze over the front hall. "You mixed two or three colors of paint to get the exact shade you wanted, Elizabeth. It was quite a project."

She turned and studied his face carefully, as though testing him for a lie. Then she withdrew her hand from his and took a long deep breath. "I do feel tired," she said. "Very tired."

He glanced at Katie. She had slumped on the bottom step, her elbows on her knees, her hands cupping her chin. When Michael met her eyes, she rolled them in an expression of frustration. He knew an eight-year-old could only comprehend so much. Why should he expect her to understand what was going on when her parents did not?

He turned back to Elizabeth. "Come on, time to get you to bed. We don't want the doctor angry with us."

Her eyes rose up the circular banister. "At least this feels right."

"Yes, the design of the stairwell has not changed. You rubbed a special oil into the oak banister and had navy carpet laid over the steps."

As they climbed the stairs, Michael glanced back to see Katie, lingering by the front door, looking worried. He winked and smiled at her, trying to indicate that everything was okay.

Although Michael paused at the master bedroom, Elizabeth continued on down the hall, automatically turning into Katie's bedroom. Feeling bewildered, Michael followed.

She stood looking around the room, that look of confusion that was starting to become a regular expression filling her face again.

"Yes, I remember this room…and yet it's different." She glanced back at Michael. "What's different about my room?"

Michael's eyes trailed over Katie's yellow bedroom. The furniture was Elizabeth's furniture, but the color scheme was different. "The carpet, drapes, and bedspread have been replaced, and yellow is Katie's favorite color, so you repainted the walls."

She nodded. "They used to be pink."

"You're right," he smiled. Now the room was a nice blend of yellow plaids and stripes with lots of teddy bears and fun posters. The dresser held an array of hair bows and Magic Markers.

Elizabeth walked across to the bedside table and opened the drawer. Katie's little white Bible was stacked on top of her Sunday school book, next to her stationery.

Elizabeth removed the Bible and stared at it for a moment; then she hugged it tightly against her chest and smiled across at Michael. "At last, I've found something that's really mine."

For a moment, Michael didn't know how to respond. Then he remembered that Elizabeth had chosen a Bible for Katie exactly like the one she had owned as a child.

She opened the cover and began to flip through the pages. "I always liked reading my Bible."

He smiled sadly at her, unable to speak, to tell her this was

Katie's room, but now it didn't seem to matter.

She sat down on the bed and looked out the window to the brawny branches of the oak tree. "I remember watching birds build their nests in that tree." She twisted around on the bed, looking at Michael with an expression of childlike wonder in her eyes.

"Once I saw a baby bird fall out of its nest and I was upset. Grandmother and I searched around the yard until we found the baby bird." Her eyes turned sad. "It was dead."

As Michael stared at her, a thought came to him, a thought so horrible he could not allow himself to dwell on it. What if Elizabeth never came out of this? What if she lingered on in this childlike state? What would happen to her? To them? To the memory of the killer stored away in some dark corner of her brain?

The man was distressed to learn that Elizabeth Calloway had been dismissed from the hospital. While she showed no signs of recognition when he tested her in the hospital, he could not press his luck. His keen instincts told him her amnesia would clear—weren't the doctors hopeful of that?

These thoughts were uppermost in his mind as he drove home from work, guiding his new BMW through the affluent, tree-lined neighborhood. Through the growing twilight, he surveyed the three-story mansions situated comfortably behind manicured lawns, the essence of prosperity. And he was the most prosperous man on the block, a thought that never failed to bring a measure of satisfaction. His money and his status were everything to him; he could not risk losing either.

Elizabeth Calloway was a greater threat than he could tolerate.

He turned his car into the driveway and roared around to

the rear of his mansion. If her memory returned—and everyone seemed optimistic that it would—she could identify him. And ruin everything.

Not only would he go to jail; all his plans for a brilliant future would go down the drain, and of course he would be ruined financially. He assumed they would sue—everyone was suing nowadays. He just couldn't let that happen to him; he had worked too hard for too long to be destroyed by one woman.

He climbed the broad steps to the back door, nodded vaguely at his household help, refusing dinner as he passed the kitchen.

"I'll be working in my office until late, so don't disturb me," he ordered.

He hurried to his spacious office and locked the door. A deep sigh escaped his chest as the safety of his retreat closed in around him. The ton of care that weighted him down began to slip away as his eyes darted toward the valuable painting, and he smiled for the first time. Behind the painting lay the wall safe where he kept his valuables. The money, the CDs, his private business papers. And of course, the white powder.

The white powder had been the source of his problem, yet it was such a sweet relief to him at times. Like now. No one knew of his cocaine habit; he had been very discreet. He prided himself on that fact as he walked to his cherry wood desk, opened a drawer, and removed from its hiding place the key to the safe.

Hurrying across the room to the painting, he carefully removed it from its prominent place on the wall and looked smugly at the small safe. The housekeeper thought he was obsessive about his paintings, not wanting them dusted or touched by anyone except professionals. In reality it was not the painting, but rather the privacy of the safe that was of utmost importance.

Turning the key, he unlocked the safe and reached into its depths, pulling his treasure from a dark corner. This was his only pleasure now. As he stared at the powder, he frowned. He must never be careless again. Only one time he had been foolish enough to leave his home under the influence of the drug. That was the night the cook had burned the roast, and he had been deluged with a sudden craving for Italian food. There was a restaurant close by; he was certain he could negotiate a couple of blocks in the Jaguar, grab a takeout dinner, and return unnoticed. But there had been the accident and now....

He couldn't think about it! His hands were already starting to shake again. He wanted it so badly—the high, the sensation of feeling good again, the relief from the mounting pressures of his job and his personal problems.

Later, after the drug had settled his nerves, he thought again of the man—the man who owed him a favor, a big favor. The man was smart, very smart, and he was one of the best at his profession.

He took a seat in the thickly cushioned desk chair and reached inside the drawer for his leather-bound address book. He would call the man, hire him to do the job, and then his concerns about Elizabeth Calloway would be over. He smiled to himself as he reached for the phone.

SIX

Michael tucked Katie in, trying to calm her fears about her mother, who now claimed Katie's room. Then he peeked in on Elizabeth.

She lay in Katie's bed, wearing a simple white cotton gown, staring blankly at the wall.

"Hi," he said, shoving his hands into his pockets and feeling a bit self-conscious as he entered the room.

"Hi." Her eyes followed him across the room, taking note of the way he sat on the edge of the white rocker beside the bed.

"Feeling any better?" he asked cheerfully.

She shrugged. "I suppose. Dinner was good. I just wasn't hungry."

Michael nodded, settling back into the chair and rocking gently. "Maybe tomorrow you'll feel more like eating. The refrigerator is full of food." His mother had left a baked ham with potato salad and coleslaw and a luscious chocolate cake. He and Katie had dived in with vigor, while Elizabeth merely picked at her food.

He tried not to stare at her now, but he felt as though an invisible wall had gone up between them. Neither knew what to say to the other, and despite his attempts to keep a positive outlook, a weary depression was pulling at the corners of his mind. He couldn't think of anything to say to his wife, and she seemed to have nothing to say to him.

Suddenly he couldn't bear the silence that grew between them, and he came to his feet, glancing down at Elizabeth. "Katie is just across the hall, and I'm in the adjoining room. If you need anything, just call."

She looked up at him, her eyes expressing gratitude. "Thanks," she said. "I'd like to leave this lamp on tonight." She indicated the small white lamp with its yellow plaid shade that sat on the bedside table.

"Fine." He hesitated, then leaned over and kissed her forehead. She made no effort to respond to his touch.

"Good night," he said hoarsely, then turned and walked out of the room.

As soon as he was in the hall, his shoulders slumped as though he had been balancing a heavy load that had shifted forward, weighing him down even more.

Would they ever return to the close marriage they had once shared, or would this invisible wall of doubt and frustration push them further apart?

He reached their bedroom and glanced helplessly around. What if Elizabeth's memory never returned? He stood in the center of their bedroom, that fear shaking him to the core of his being. His eyes trailed over the bedroom, filled with mementos of their life together: framed snapshots of them at various stages of courtship and marriage, their wedding portrait in its gold frame, hanging in the center of the wall. The portrait featured a beautiful bride in a white satin dress that cascaded about her slim figure. Her blonde head was tilted back as she looked lovingly at the bridegroom. Michael stared at this younger version of himself, lean and tanned in a white tux. He was grinning from ear to ear. The happy couple blurred as tears filled his eyes.

Just when they had reunited, discovering an even greater joy in marriage after being separated, life had thrown them another curve ball. Never in a million years could he have imagined anything so bizarre, so horrible, as the problem that faced them now.

He sank onto the foot of the canopied cherry wood bed and let the pain wash over him. It was a relief to give way to it after keeping up the brave face to so many.

"God, help us," he prayed, his broken voice the only sound in the depressing stillness of the bedroom. "You're the only one who can help us now."

And he knew this was absolutely true.

Elizabeth could not get to sleep. She felt oddly alone and left out of the family circle here, as though she had never really belonged. The house did not bring the welcome she had hoped for, and her memory stretched no further than her early childhood. She had tried to hide her disappointment from Michael and Katie, but she could tell from the worried glances and curious looks that they were disappointed as well. This merely added to her frustration.

As the bedside lamp bathed the room in a soft glow, she opened the drawer of the night stand and reached inside for the white Bible.

For a moment she hugged it against her chest, wishing that she could magically open the pages and find the answers to all the questions she faced about her life. Maybe she could.

Blinking, she opened its cover and flipped through the pages. A ribboned bookmark protruded from the center of the Bible. Carefully, she turned to the page where the bookmark rested. Psalms. Her eyes fell on the twenty-third chapter and she began to read, taking comfort in its message. Feeling better, she read the chapter again, then stared into space. She felt as though she had just emerged from the valley of the shadow of death, had even been touched by that shadow. Yet God had been with her, sparing her life, uniting her with her loved ones.

Tears of gratitude filled her eyes and slipped down her cheeks.

God, let me be a part of this family again, she prayed, unaware that her husband in the adjoining bedroom was praying a similar prayer.

The next morning, the sound of voices from somewhere in the house awakened Elizabeth. It was a woman's voice, speaking loud and shrill, complaining that the house was too hot.

Elizabeth frowned, carefully hoisting her legs to the side of the bed, always mindful to move slowly lest she provoke the pain in her head. She reached for the white cotton housecoat that matched her gown, pushing her arms through the sleeves as the woman's voice droned on. For a minute it seemed that no one would answer her. Then, as Elizabeth pushed her feet into her slippers and reached for the bedpost to steady herself, she heard the low tones of Michael, her husband, responding to the woman's incessant whine.

Walking shakily toward the doorway, the housecoat swirling about her slim legs, she located the direction of the voices. They were coming from the hall below her, and she made her way slowly toward the stairs.

The woman continued to complain, and by now Elizabeth had recognized the voice. It was her mother. What was she doing here? And why was she fussing at Michael?

As she reached the stairs, the walls seemed to dip and sway about her. She wound her arms around the banister, hugging the wood for support. In a few seconds, her head began to clear. She took a deep breath and with a firm grip on the banister, she carefully made her way down the carpeted stairs. As she reached the landing, she could see the heads of three people beneath the crystal chandelier.

It was her mother, Franklin, and Michael. She blinked, bringing the rest of their bodies into view as she continued on down the stairs. The couple stood just inside the front door, facing Michael. Her mother was flinging her jeweled hands around as she spoke, and now Elizabeth realized how nervous the woman made her.

"Are you really satisfied with this Dr. Cope's credentials?" she demanded, glaring at Michael. She was dressed in a blue linen suit and navy pumps, and even at this early hour wore makeup and pearls around her neck, as though she were off to a garden party.

"Millicent," Michael spoke firmly, "you aren't helping us by looking on the dark side of everything. We need to work together on this and—"

"But you won't allow us to work together," Millicent cut him off. "You've brought her back here to the country, away from the doctors and hospitals. And what about her safety?"

Suddenly, all the years of listening to this woman's complaints brought a flash of anger to Elizabeth. How dare her mother storm in here and try to take control when she was an adult with a husband and a child!

"Mother." Her voice sliced the air, bringing a moment of stunned silence.

All heads swiveled upward.

"We're doing just fine," Elizabeth snapped, glaring down at her mother. She was conscious of Michael coming up the stairs to her side, but her eyes never left the couple below. "Furthermore, I'm getting tired of hearing you attack my husband. It seems to me he's making the right choices. Why do you insist on nagging him?"

Millicent gasped loudly. The blood drained from her face as she tilted her head back to stare incredulously at Elizabeth.

Franklin fidgeted uncomfortably, a flush rising up his neck.

Since her mother seemed to be in shock, Elizabeth realized it must not be her habit to storm out at her mother. But she was sick and tired of her complaints; she wondered how Michael had managed to keep his temper.

He was at her side, his arm steadying her. "Let me help you down the stairs."

"Well," Millicent said, finally finding her voice, "it's obvious that we are not welcome here. Even my granddaughter has been unfriendly."

"I'm friendly." Katie's head popped around a doorway. "I just don't want to go shopping with you." Her head disappeared again.

"Mother," Elizabeth sighed, "why don't you give us some time to adjust?" Her eyes moved to Franklin, who had stepped closer to his wife, looking at her with concern. "Why don't you and Franklin go back to..." *Where had they come from?* Elizabeth wondered suddenly. She decided it didn't matter. "Why don't you let us come visit you later?"

Tears filled Millicent's blue eyes and her wide shoulders began to heave. "In other words, get out!"

"That's not what I said," Elizabeth replied shakily, suddenly wondering if she could really handle this situation after all.

"It's what you meant," Millicent said, yanking the front door open. "Come on, Franklin."

For a moment, the man hesitated, as though torn between making some statement or placating his wife. His shoulders shrugged lightly against his dark business suit as he turned and trudged out the door.

"Wait, Millicent." Michael left Elizabeth and rushed to the door.

She could hear him talking in low tones out on the front

porch, assuring her mother that he would stay in touch, keep her informed.

Elizabeth heard no reply, merely the sound of footsteps crossing the porch, down the steps, and then car doors slamming.

She sighed and turned to go back up the stairs. The scene had exhausted her. It occurred to her that she should go down and visit with Michael and Katie, but she didn't feel up to it. She wanted to hide in the yellow room again and shut out the sounds of fear and worry.

Michael spent the morning on the phone getting an update from Jay, which amounted to very little. There was no progress in the investigation; nothing new had been turned up.

He called his office, instructing his secretary, Anita, to take messages and phone him if anything important came up. Then he pulled out a legal pad and his silver pen and began to jot down names of other investigators he knew who might be able to help them.

After a while, he pushed the pad aside in frustration and dropped the pen on the desk. What was he doing? In his heart, he knew no one would do a better job than Jay. Furthermore, he and Jay knew more about the case than anyone else. He trusted Jay's instincts as well as his own. Both were good detectives; both possessed a keen understanding of people and how they reacted in various situations.

He had a suspicion about the man who had killed two people and left Elizabeth for dead. He was not some known criminal on the run; he was a man too frightened to come forward and admit what he had done. He didn't know why he kept circling back to this conclusion, but he did. And Jay seemed to feel the same way, no matter how many times other possibilities were suggested to them.

He stood, stretching his arms over his head. From the kitchen, he heard Katie talking to her mother. He decided it was time to check on Elizabeth.

He was still amazed that she had argued her mother down, had taken a firm stand for him and Katie. Secretly he was pleased, and yet, despite his differences with Millicent, he was sorry to see her so hurt. She had dissolved in tears once she reached the porch, unable to say more to Michael.

Elizabeth's memory seemed to be clearing where her mother was concerned. Maybe in time he and Katie would come in focus.

"Building blocks," he mumbled to himself, then felt vaguely irritated that he had started to mumble in his frustration.

Building blocks, he mentally repeated, recalling what the neurologist had told them. Her memory would start coming back in layers, building the foundation of her life and working upward. He kept quoting that phrase to Elizabeth and to him- self, and somehow it kept him from panicking.

Elizabeth had finally dressed in shorts and a T-shirt and was seated at the kitchen table, drinking a glass of lemonade. She had been listening to Katie detail her plans for the coming school year. When Michael searched Elizabeth's face, he saw only a little-girl kind of wonder there. He prayed that Katie thought her mother was clinging to her every word, rather than trying to remember giving birth to her.

"You girls ready for some lunch?" he asked, striding toward the refrigerator.

"I'm not hungry," Elizabeth began.

"Mom," Katie scolded, "you always want me to eat at meal-time."

"Oh," Elizabeth replied to Katie's outburst. The word was becoming a mantra for her, Michael thought, a word that neither gave her away nor revealed what she remembered.

"Now it's your turn to eat," Katie said, assuming the role of boss.

Michael gave Katie a look but failed to catch her eye. He wanted to signal to her to ease up. She was beginning to reveal a typically childish impatience toward her mother.

But then Elizabeth unfolded her napkin in her lap, preparing to eat, and Michael decided maybe Katie's bossing would accomplish more than his.

SEVEN

Lieutenant Wilkens sat beside Michael and Elizabeth at the kitchen table the next afternoon. All three of them looked hopeful and eager. The mug shots that Wilkens had brought up to Oak Shadows lay stacked in a neat pile, all seventy-eight of them. These were possible suspects: past offenders, drug dealers who could afford sports cars, some who actually drove black sports cars.

I'll find him here, Elizabeth told herself. *I'll know him when I see him.*

Patiently, she began to look through the black-and-white glossies. Some of the faces appeared to be normal, others held a look of evil about their eyes.

One by one, she studied each face, waiting for some kind of recognition to dawn in her mind. Nothing came. She studied the features—flat noses, pug noses, normal noses—amazing, some part of her brain told her. No two people were similar, but some of the features were similar. All were known criminals.

What have they done? she wanted to ask. In the background, the ticking of the clock on the kitchen wall began to grate on her nerves. Her forehead started to throb when she was halfway through the stack.

Try to remember; you can remember, she told herself. But in truth her memory stretched no further than her childhood here at Oak Shadows. Actually, she was starting to feel more like a teenager; even Katie had commented on her ponytail.

Painstakingly, she studied each picture, her forehead drawn in concentration, her fingers trembling as she reached the last picture. Michael stood beside her, ever protective, trying to be gentle with her.

After she had finished looking at the last picture, she turned to both of them and shook her head, feeling miserable that she was so little help. "I'm sorry. I would help if I could. I just don't remember ever seeing any of these people."

Silence filled the kitchen. Then Lt. Wilkens spoke up.

"Mrs. Calloway, I don't want to push you," he said, looking pained about something, "but the family of the other victims is really pressuring us."

Elizabeth stared at him. "Michael said there was another car involved, but what—?" She looked from Michael to Lt. Wilkens, obviously confused.

Lt. Wilkens sighed. "Michael, there's a limit to how long you can shield her. Surely you understand Mr. Cunningham's situation?"

Michael nodded. "And we sympathize completely. But until my wife's amnesia clears—"

"Wait a minute!" Elizabeth put up her hand to stop Michael. "Lt. Wilkens, what do you mean by Mr. Cunningham's *situation?* What's wrong with him?"

Lt. Wilkens looked at Michael, and Michael reached for Elizabeth's hand. "Well, you see…"

Elizabeth could tell he was trying to speak gently about something that was crucial, something she should know.

"What is it?" she demanded.

"Abbot Cunningham wants to find the man whose car hit the Cunningham car."

"There's more," she said, frowning at him, "and I resent your not telling me."

"Okay. His wife and son were in the other car that was hit. They…died," Michael sighed.

Elizabeth gasped, horrified. Tears filled her eyes and poured down her cheeks as she shook her head in helpless frustration. "And I can't help."

She could feel Michael's arm around her shoulders as she sobbed the words. He lifted her out of the chair.

Lt. Wilkens stood and gave her a sad smile. "You did your best, Mrs. Calloway. I'll tell Mr. Cunningham."

"And she can look at more mug shots," Michael pointed out.

But what good will it do? Elizabeth thought miserably. *If I can't remember my husband and daughter, how can I remember some stranger I glimpsed for only a few seconds?*

Her heart was racing, her head was spinning, even her breathing seemed erratic.

"Come on," Michael urged her gently, "you need to lie down."

"I need more than that," Elizabeth snapped, then shook her head. "Sorry, I shouldn't be cross with you. You are trying so hard to help me. It's just that…" She didn't know what else to say as they climbed the steps together.

Michael said nothing more, and Elizabeth fought the urge to complete her sentence. Could she be helped? she wondered. If only someone could wave a magic wand and instantly restore her memory. So many problems would be solved, or at least the people involved could work at solving the problems.

Once they reached the yellow room, she sank gratefully on the bed and looked helplessly at Michael.

"What's going to happen?" she asked bleakly.

"We're going to take this one day at a time. And we'll conquer each day."

Listening to his voice, Elizabeth thought he sounded so sure. If only she could feel more confident!

"Thanks for being so understanding," she said, leaning against him as he lifted her feet up to the bed and smoothed her hair back from her face.

"It will get better," he promised before he turned and walked out of the room.

She wondered if he really believed that, or was he just giving her hope?

She closed her eyes and gave way to the weariness that claimed her. Again, she sought refuge in sleep.

Michael's confident demeanor lasted only until he closed Elizabeth's door. He had been so hopeful that one of those pictures would bring a memory to her…that she would see the face of the driver who had hit her and killed two innocent people. But she had not.

He returned to the kitchen, trying to think what to say to Lt. Wilkens. He found him seated at the kitchen table, staring glumly at the mug shots.

Michael cleared his throat, glancing down at the pictures. "I think we have to face the fact that the man we're looking for may simply be a well-to-do citizen here in Atlanta."

"But where's the car?"

Michael shook his head, staring into space. "I don't know."

There seemed to be nothing left to say. The car had not been found, nor any witnesses, and for now, the investigation had hit a dead end until Elizabeth remembered something that could help them.

"Michael, do you think your wife should see another specialist?" Wilkens asked suddenly. "It's been a week."

Michael plunged his hands through his hair, trying to vent the frustration that continued to mount within him.

"Yeah, maybe. The neurologist feels she is making a little progress, but this isn't getting us very far."

Lt. Wilkens sighed, and Michael saw that he was looking at him differently. Sympathetically. "Well, she's alive, Michael. And maybe tomorrow it will all come back to her. Who knows?"

"Yeah, let's hope so." Michael took a deep breath, glancing through the kitchen window to a bright sunny day. "Because she's as healthy as she is, I've developed patience I never had before. As for Cunningham—" he turned back to Lt. Wilkens, feeling awful—"tell the poor guy this thing has torn our family apart."

He hadn't planned to be so honest about his private life, but he wanted the department to understand that they were living a nightmare. "Elizabeth sleeps in Katie's room, Katie sleeps in the guest room, and I sleep alone in the master bedroom," he continued. "Elizabeth's mother and I have had our differences because she thinks I'm not doing enough to help Elizabeth. Then Elizabeth practically ordered her out of the house. Or at least her mother took it that way."

Millicent had phoned last night, asking to speak to Katie.

"Your mother didn't mean what she said to me," Millicent had reported to Katie. "I'm afraid she's been influenced by your father."

"Daddy didn't do anything," Katie retaliated. "I think you're being mean."

Upon hearing that, Michael had quickly taken the phone and tried to calm Millicent, but again she was in tears.

"Is there anything we can do?" Lt. Wilkens broke through his muddled thoughts.

Michael shrugged. "Just find the guy. As for us, everyone is praying for Elizabeth and trying to help her. Mom keeps reminding us that God will work things out in time. The waiting is the worst part."

Lt. Wilkens shook his head, looking thoughtfully at Michael. He turned and gathered the mug shots. "Well, I must get back to town."

Michael sighed. "I'm sorry we didn't accomplish anything. I appreciate your making the trip out here."

The older man sighed. "No problem. Maybe we'll get a break."

"Maybe we will." Michael nodded, wishing with all of his heart for that to be true.

EIGHT

The next morning, Elizabeth sat in the white rocking chair near the window overlooking the oak tree. The rocker didn't fit her anymore; it seemed to have shrunk. That didn't matter. She loved sitting here, looking out at the tree.

Her eyes dropped to the white Bible in her lap. She picked it up, holding it to her chest. Perhaps if she read it, cover to cover, it would bring back images that were missing and help to restore her memory.

Her memory. A terrible ache filled her heart as she thought about the man who had lost his wife and child in the car accident. She needed to help him; more than anything she wanted to remember for herself.

She swallowed hard; it would do no good to cry again. She had shed enough tears yesterday after Michael took her upstairs.

She forced herself to think about what the doctor had said—that she'd have a better chance of recovering her memory if she were not stressed. She had to keep her mind relaxed.

She turned to the book of Psalms. The chapters were beautiful, but she was drawn to them for another reason. It had something to do with the present, of that she was sure. But first she would have to start with Genesis. She smoothed down the page and began to read.

A thought struck her, filling her with hope. She could still read! She looked out the window and smiled with deep satisfaction. A cardinal had dipped down to light on the branch of the oak tree. Now the red bird cocked his head and looked curiously at her.

Grandmother's words leaped into her mind—a single flash yet it was clear and poignant to her now. She could see her grandmother's face, as clearly as if she stood in the room beside her and spoke the words: *If a cardinal flies close to you or crosses your path, that's a sign of good luck.*

The words echoed through Elizabeth's mind. Then the picture faded.

"All right, Grandmother," she whispered, "I'll expect a flash of good luck."

She smiled for a moment, feeling better. Then she picked up the Bible and something fell out of the back. She reached down to pick it up and saw that it was a thin bookmark with pink tassels.

She examined the bookmark carefully. Across the front there was a picture of an eagle soaring through a beautiful sky. Underneath the picture was a verse: "But those who hope in the LORD will renew their strength. They will soar on wings like eagles; they will run and not grow weary, they will walk and not be faint. Isaiah 40:31"

"Hi, Mom." Katie stood in the door of the bedroom.

"Hello." Elizabeth smiled at her.

"What are you reading?" Katie asked, wandering over to the chair to glance down at the page in the Bible.

Elizabeth looked blankly at the page.

"Oh, you found your bookmark!" Katie exclaimed, picking up the bookmark and turning it over. "This bookmark is special to you," she said, glancing from the bookmark to her mom. "You gave me one just like it."

Elizabeth stared at the message. "Yes," she said, remembering that it had once been very important to her, but she wasn't sure when or why. However, the words were lovely, and she found herself thinking of those words now. "Hope in the Lord," she sighed. "I guess that's what I'm doing now."

Katie reached out and hugged her. "You told me it works for you."

"I did?" Elizabeth smiled sadly, having no memory of the conversation whatsoever.

"I think the bookmark was something Dad put in your Christmas stocking one year. That's what you told me."

"Oh." She read the message on the back of the bookmark: *It's been a tough year, but with God's help, we have made it.*

Elizabeth stared at the message. What did that mean? Maybe she would ask Michael.

"Mom," Katie began. She had wandered across the room. "Last year you and Dad put this candle in my stocking. It was just one of the fun things you gave me." Katie stood beside an oak table, pointing to a candle in a cute little jar.

Elizabeth stared at the jar, trying desperately to remember the significance.

"Remember," Katie prompted, "it's a sugar cookie candle. I can get Dad to light it." She ran to the door and yelled for her dad.

Elizabeth could hear footsteps echoing down the hall. Soon, the man she was growing to like very much appeared in the door.

"Hey, you two!" he called.

"Dad, will you light my candle? I want Mom to smell it."

Elizabeth looked from Michael to Katie. She really hadn't asked to have it lighted, but she tried to smile in agreement, wanting to be pleasant.

"Sure," he said, walking over to the mantel and removing a box of matches. "By the way, Katie, I'm proud of you for never attempting to do this yourself. You know it's against the rules."

Katie grinned. "Oh, Daddy," she said, pretending to pout.

Then she giggled. "You and Mom said I could burn the house down."

"Or burn your hand," he called over his shoulder as he lit the candle.

A delicious fragrance began to fill the room, and suddenly a vision came to Elizabeth. She was in the kitchen, shaping white dough with her hands. She remembered the texture of the dough. It was soft and creamy.

"Sugar cookies," she said, staring into space.

"Mom! You remember us making cookies!" Katie squealed with delight.

Elizabeth turned her eyes toward the flickering light of the candle, entranced. She wasn't sure who was in the kitchen with her, but it made Katie happy to think it was she, so Elizabeth merely turned to her and smiled again.

"That's great," Michael said, leaning down to plant a kiss on the top of Katie's head. "Katie, that was smart of you to think of that."

Katie was kneeling beside the rocking chair, her blue eyes twinkling as she turned her face up to her mother.

"Want to light the angel candle?" Michael asked.

"Oh, cool!" Katie jumped to her feet. "I forgot about that one."

Elizabeth's eyes followed Michael across the room to another candle. This one sat on the mantel behind her, and it was very pretty.

"Mom, what do you think of when you see the angel candle?" Katie inquired, watching her mother in fascination as though they were playing some kind of little game.

The angel candle.

Elizabeth stared up at the small jar with the angel imprint on the front.

Angels. She could see another angel, a small one dressed in white with a halo over her head. The little angel was perched on top of a tree.

"A tree," she said slowly, thoughtfully. And then another vision flashed through her mind. The tree held strings of lights; some of the lights seemed to bubble; others blinked. And balls. Shiny green balls.

"Our Christmas tree," Katie squealed, running over to hug her father. Elizabeth stared at them wistfully. The joy Katie seemed to feel was not quite reflected in Michael's eyes. He was more thoughtful as he studied Elizabeth carefully.

She wondered if he knew she saw only the tree, that nobody was standing there. Not these two people, not anyone. It was just a beautiful tree.

Suddenly she felt tired, so tired that she could scarcely keep her eyes open. And her head was beginning to ache again. She placed her elbow on the armrest of the rocker and cradled the side of her head with her hand. She could hardly keep her eyes open.

"Katie, I think your mom needs to rest now. You know how you used to go to sleep smelling the candles until I came to your room and put out the flame."

Katie nodded but said nothing. When Elizabeth lifted her head and glanced toward Katie, she saw that the blue eyes were narrowed suspiciously.

"I think your mom feels the way you did; that smell always made you sleepy. Why don't we let her rest?"

"I'm sorry," Elizabeth managed to say as Katie's mouth drooped. "I didn't rest well last night."

Katie heaved a deep sigh and flounced out of the room. Elizabeth had a feeling that Katie was disappointed in her, but she couldn't help it. She was so tired she could barely sit up.

Michael came over and helped her from the chair to the bed.

"It's okay." Michael's voice was smooth and reassuring. "We understand."

When Elizabeth was comfortably situated in the bed, she closed her eyes, giving way to utter exhaustion. The aching in her head was diminishing, however, and she lay very still. Somewhere down the hall, she could hear Katie's voice, snapping with irritation.

"Dad, she doesn't really know us," Katie said. "She's just pretending. I *hate* it when she pretends! You said she had to get her strength back. How long does that take?" Her voice rose, drifting distinctly to Elizabeth's ears before Michael mumbled something in a quiet, low voice.

Elizabeth curled in a ball, sobbing quietly. She was a disappointment to everyone. She couldn't help with the investigation, she didn't feel like a wife or a mother, she only felt like...like a little girl. And the worst part was that nobody seemed to understand. She cried softly into her pillow, finally giving way to exhaustion.

When she awoke, the house was quiet. She got out of bed and wandered back to the rocking chair, picking up the Bible she had left there.

Again, she opened the book to the Psalms. She seemed to feel a special comfort just holding the Bible, turning its pages. She liked the twenty-third chapter of Psalms, and now she read it aloud, trying to absorb every word.

Even though I walk through the valley of the shadow of death, I will fear no evil....

She stopped reading and stared out the window, thinking. She had been close to death, she knew that, and yet God had brought her back to life, back to her family. *But she didn't remember these people*. The woman who was foremost in her mind was not here. She had seen her portrait in its gold frame downstairs, but everyone looked sad when she asked about her grandmother.

She frowned. She didn't like her mother; there had always been conflict between them, she knew that much. But in the earlier days, there had been Grandmother to soothe away the difficulties. And now she was gone.

Elizabeth picked up the Bible again, holding it to her chest. There was a link here to her past and her present. She didn't know how she knew that but she did. This had been her Bible as a child—perhaps if she read it, cover to cover, it would help to restore her memory.

She smoothed down the pages and began to read Psalms.

NINE

In the sunlight that shingled through the pine branches overhead, the man studied the map he had drawn of the Calloway property. He was on an adjoining farm approximately a quarter mile away from their land. Here there was a thick stretch of woods that provided a natural hiding place. He had marked a vantage spot where the land rose slightly, and by climbing a tree he could get a clear view of the front of the Calloway house.

He had driven past the property and spotted an undercover agent pretending to be a farmer working on a piece of machinery in the field. The man was not fooled. He knew the house would be under surveillance. Such an obvious surveillance amused him.

He had changed trucks and caps each time he passed, and the man continued to work on the machinery. The man knew the agent was stationed near the road to keep watch on passing vehicles, and he had not fallen for it. The Calloways' watchdogs mistook him for a fool, and he was nothing if not cautious.

Obviously, gaining access to the house was not going to be easy. The gate was locked. Calloway's car was there, and he had no way of knowing how many agents were inside the house.

After studying his map and weighing his options, he knew the woods would be the best choice for his hiding place.

A rapping on the door frame brought her attention to Michael, standing in the doorway and smiling across the room at her.

"Want to take a walk?"

She laid down the Bible and got up slowly. The dizziness still came and went, but at least the attacks were farther apart.

"Sure."

"It's a beautiful day, and I thought some fresh air and sunshine might be good for you."

She nodded. "Okay." She slipped her bare feet into loafers and got up, glancing at her reflection in the dresser mirror. She was wearing shorts and a T-shirt, and her hair was pulled back in a ponytail. When she turned to Michael, he was watching her curiously.

"I saw all these ribbons and I just had a notion to put my hair up in a ponytail," she said, waving at Katie's array of ribbons on the dresser.

He merely nodded.

"By the way, where is Katie?" she asked. She felt terrible that she did not have a clear memory of her daughter, but Michael kept reassuring her things would soon start to make sense.

"Brooke came to visit." He reached for her arm and slipped his fingers in hers as they walked down the stairs together. "They're out in the backyard, so this is a good time for us to go outside."

Once they stepped out onto the wide porch, Elizabeth took a deep breath and immediately felt better. "It's lovely here, isn't it?"

Michael nodded. "You know, you had a hard time convincing me to leave the city and move back out here when you inherited this place. I was stubborn." He winked at her.

Elizabeth stared at him for a moment. She was not thinking so much of what he said, but how attractive he was. She could see why she had married him, for he had great appeal to her. And she could feel herself being drawn to him in a physical way. She dropped her eyes suddenly, not knowing how to feel about that. About anything.

"You were right, of course," he continued smoothly, as though unaware she was having thoughts of him. "It feels so good here, so peaceful," he said, taking a deep breath.

As they walked along together, Michael felt himself begin to relax. The past two weeks had taken their toll. Could it really have been only two weeks? It seemed impossible. He felt he had aged ten years, that his world had been turned upside down with the accident, that their life might never be the same.

Elizabeth studied the yard. It was different now from the way she remembered it. She could not analyze what was different about it. It just was. Her eyes came to rest on a fountain in a corner of the yard. It surprised her.

"The fountain?" Elizabeth turned back to Michael, that look of confusion filling her eyes.

He followed her gaze across at the fountain and began to smile. "Remember you and I found that old fountain at a flea market in Snellville? We bought it for a song and dragged it home. Then you spent the next week polishing it up."

They walked toward it, feeling the cooling spray of the water tumbling over a small rock bed.

"You were so proud of the final results," he said from behind her. She nodded absently, then turned toward something in the corner of the yard.

"The birdhouse!" she cried, clasping her hands together as she stared up at the bird house perched on a wooden pole. Each time she remembered something it was as though someone had given her a special gift. She stood gazing up at the birdhouse, old and weathered.

"We cleared the weeds out from around this corner of the yard here," Michael patiently explained as he stood beside her, pointing to something nearby. "Remember how surprised I was to find the smooth rock seat made from fieldstone?"

She nodded, turning toward the seat. She sat down, and a slow smile began to creep over her mouth. She nodded at him, and he knew that she was remembering something. He hurried to her side, to sit down on the rock with her.

"Grandmother and I used to sit here and watch the birds. She kept a bird book in the study, and she taught me about all the different kinds of birds. I can recall that part very clearly now; the little red birds were my favorite."

"Good! You see, things are coming back just as I promised you. Sit here for just a minute. I want to get something."

Elizabeth watched his tall frame striding across the lawn. He was wearing Levi's, a polo shirt, tennis shoes, and socks. She liked to see him dress casually like that, rather than in his business suits. Somehow it made her feel more at home. Her eyes ran down her own shirt and shorts, and she wondered if she had liked dressing this way before the accident. She had seen some very nice suits and dresses hanging in the master bedroom, with matching shoes and handbags. Somehow she wouldn't feel right dressed like that now; she wanted to wear things more…playful.

Soon he came out the front door, bounding down the steps and crossing the lawn to her again. He held something in his hand.

"I wanted to show you a photo album." He sat down beside her on the rock. "We went to Cancún on our honeymoon."

"Did we have a big wedding?"

He grinned and shook his head. "Too big to suit me, but you were beautiful in your white dress. Maybe we'll look at that photo album next and talk about our wedding."

As she looked into his blue eyes and saw the glow of excitement, she wondered how she was supposed to react to him. She didn't feel like his wife. He was just a friend to her now, nothing more.

He was opening the album. "Here, look at these pictures."

Elizabeth looked down at the open book, focusing on a series of photographs. She and Michael were standing on the beach, their arms around one another. They looked very happy, very young. She stared at the picture for a long time and suddenly something started to nag at the back of her mind. Something about her skin.

She blinked at the two-piece floral swimsuit she was wearing; then she looked up at Michael.

"It was hot," she said slowly, feeling a warmth on her skin. "Very hot there."

"That's right!" Michael's eyes widened. "It was extremely hot the week we were there."

Elizabeth smiled at him and looked back at the picture. "My skin, something about my skin...."

"You got sunburned!" he exclaimed. "The first day we were there. We stayed in the sun too long." He began to rub her arm gently. "Remember afterwards we spent most of our time inside buildings. Shopping. You loved looking at the handmade items. And remember I bought you a special ring?"

"A special ring."

"Yes, it was silver."

Elizabeth reached up and touched his cheek. His blue eyes glowed with happiness. That one memory had encouraged him so much.

Tears filled her eyes and slipped down her cheeks. "I'm so sorry. I want so badly to remember, to feel the way you do.

And I do feel something, something very strong." Her voice fell, she dropped her eyes. "But I don't know what it is."

Elizabeth knew he was disappointed, but she didn't know what to do or say about their relationship. They had apparently been very much in love and she couldn't remember it. She liked him very much, and she wanted to tell him so, but she felt certain it would be a disappointment to him to hear the word *like* rather than *love*.

Why had this happened to her? Why *her*?

"Let's look at the rest of the pictures," Michael said, flipping the pages.

She saw more photographs of them together, frolicking in the aquamarine waves, standing before a beautiful hotel with Mediterranean style architecture. There was a picture of Michael, then a picture of Michael in a black velvet sombrero with her posing, head tilted, in a crazy feathered hat. They looked like they were having so much fun together. As she stared at the glossy photographs, she tried desperately to remember something about their honeymoon. But all she remembered was her skin…and something more…something about Michael. She looked up at him, puzzled.

"Elizabeth, I was wondering if…"

She leaned forward, wondering why he was hesitating.

"If what?"

Michael shoved his hands in his pockets and let his eyes drift over the lawn, then return slowly to her. "Well, I was wondering if you would like to go down to Cancún for a few days. We could stay in the same hotel, swim and lie in the sun. You remember you loved playing in the waves?"

Elizabeth frowned, staring down at the pictures again. She could see the woman was a younger version of herself. And in those pictures, she smiled up at Michael as though she adored him.

She looked at the man standing beside her now, years older yet still very handsome and caring and…hopeful. He was her husband! These blank spaces in her mind were so unfair to him, to Katie, even to her.

She stared at the couple in the picture who looked so happy, so in love.

"Maybe it's not a good idea," Michael said with a heavy sigh, reaching for the photo album.

She held on to it. "No, wait." She turned another page and saw a picture of the ocean at sunset. "This is really beautiful," she said, considering his suggestion more seriously. "Let me think about it."

He nodded. "Fair enough."

Coming home to Oak Shadows had brought back her childhood; maybe if she went with Michael to this place, the trip would restore her memories of their special time together. And she would feel married again. She wanted more than anything to piece together the blank spaces in her mind.

"Maybe we *should* go," she said, somewhat tentatively. Glancing from the happy couple in the photo album to the man standing beside her, she began to nod. "It's worth a try. I'm willing to go if the doctor thinks it's okay for me to travel."

Michael looked surprised. "Really? Well…good. *Great!* First, I'll call the doctor and get his opinion. If he thinks it's a good idea, I'll start making hotel and plane reservations."

He squeezed her hand. "It'll be fun, Elizabeth. And I think a change will do us both good."

She looked up at him and smiled, feeling a glow of excitement that she hadn't felt before. Maybe things were starting to come back to her.

"Now come on," he said, pulling her up from the seat, "let's go check on our daughter."

Laying the scrapbook on a small table, they walked around to the backyard, watching as Katie and Brooke perfected their routine.

"They both want to be mascots for the junior high cheerleading team this fall," Michael said, looking slightly amused as he watched the girls, "and they're spotting each other on handstands and flips."

As they watched, Michael shook his head. Katie had just hit the ground again and pulled herself up, looking frustrated, while Brooke bolted right into a backflip.

"Katie's still a little awkward," Michael commented.

Elizabeth made no reply as they silently watched. "Brooke is taller than Katie," she noted, "and more muscular. I guess that's why it's easier for her." She turned back to Michael. "It makes me a little nervous to watch them. Could we look at some more pictures? I think it helps more than anything to look at photographs."

"Sure!" Michael slipped his hand around hers, and they walked back around to the seat in the front yard. "I just had an idea. Let me grab another album that might interest you more."

Elizabeth waited as he bounded up the steps and inside the house. The pictures pulled at her mind, restoring her life in bits and pieces. Soon he was back out the door, another album in hand.

"Here, we'll start at the beginning of this one. You made it years ago."

He opened the cover. It was a fun book, with lots of silly captions done in all forms of calligraphy above and below the photographs.

"These were two of your sidekicks, Betsy and Lisa."

She stared at the picture. The three girls were playing volleyball, presenting a study in contrasts. Elizabeth was medium height, slim and blonde, while one girl was a tiny brunette and the other a tall redhead. In the picture they were smiling as though they were having fun.

Something flashed in Elizabeth's mind. "I kept missing the ball. I was not good at volleyball." She looked at Michael questioningly, as though he must approve her answer.

"You used to tell me you were uncoordinated in everything except cheerleading."

Suddenly a crazy cheer echoed through her mind and she spoke it aloud, laughing as she did.

"Two bits, four bits, six bits a dollar, all for Jackets, stand up and holler!"

"Yeaaa," Michael yelled, clapping. "You're right on target."

She was seized with excitement and fun. Eagerly, she scanned the photos on the continuing pages. There were numerous pictures of friends: lounging on beach towels at the beach, posing in crazy hats at some tourist shop, grouped together around a campfire. Her eyes paused on the next page of photographs.

"The Smokies." She stared at the picture. "A place called…" She began to snap her fingers, as though the gesture would speed up her thoughts.

"I'm not going to tell you," Michael said, grinning. "You have to remember."

She turned to another picture at the same location. She was standing on a large rock, poised against the backdrop of sprawling mountains. She leaned over to study the picture. The mountains towered up into a cloudy haze, and yet the scene was breathtakingly beautiful. She looked at the other girl standing beside her in the next picture.

"Sheilah! That was her name. But she and I were always disagreeing. I didn't like the busy tourist areas," she said slowly, staring intently at the pictures. She pointed to a heavyset girl with her mouth fixed in a pouting line. "She didn't want to go to the place I chose."

"And where was that?" Michael inquired.

Her mind was a blank. Then, ever so slowly, images started to unfold. Some place out of the way, some place that she adored while Betsy and Sheilah tugged at her to go back to…

"Gatlinburg!" she exclaimed. "We were in Gatlinburg."

"Great!" Michael's eyes were shining. "Now, remember this place?"

He turned the page to a quaint little town with mountains scalloped against the horizon.

She bit her lip, trying hard to dredge up a name. "I loved that place, I know that," she said. "But I feel like pulling my hair out in frustration."

The frustration was mounting. She didn't want to play this game anymore. But then Michael spoke up, piquing her interest again.

"I'll give you a hint. You have a fascination for angels. Not just the one on the candle, or the one on the tree; you like to go to a place that sells lots of angels in different forms of handicraft."

"Angel Valley!" she cried, and again tears sprang into her eyes. "Oh, Michael, I'm getting better, aren't I?"

He touched her cheek tenderly. "Yes, darling, you are."

"But my memory is coming in bits and pieces. There's no continuity to anything."

"It will come," he said, looking at her with hope-filled eyes.

Elizabeth smiled, knowing she had made him happy.

The man stashed his truck on an old logging road that paralleled the back side of the adjoining farm. He was forced to walk half a mile through the woods, even though his leg had begun to ache from the old injury. Slowly, he followed the map until he reached the slight incline. There, he located an oak tree he could climb, one with a stable branch where he could sit, shielded by the heavy leaves. When at last he was positioned, he sighed with relief. He could watch the house and he would be patient.

Later in the day, his patience was rewarded when Michael and Elizabeth Calloway sauntered to the front yard. They took a seat in a far corner and were looking at something. His eyes swept over the grounds—the house, front and back. There was no one in sight. He felt that jolt of electricity that always came to him when the moment was right.

He had a clear view of her now. He positioned the rifle against his shoulder, pressed his cheek against the stock, and looked through the tiny lenses. Her head was centered in the crosshairs. His finger crept to the trigger.

TEN

J ay raced up the driveway in his Ford LTD, the blue light flashing on his dashboard. He screeched to a halt and jumped out, spotting Elizabeth and Michael seated in a corner of the yard.

When they saw him approaching, they both stood and began to walk quickly toward him. Something was obviously wrong.

"Michael, I need to speak to you inside. Police business." Jay cast a quick grin at Elizabeth, hoping she was fooled.

"Is it about the…man?" she asked worriedly.

"It's about *a* man," Jay responded, automatically looking around the grounds. "Let's go inside."

Walking close to Elizabeth, Jay rushed the couple up the sidewalk and into the house.

The man in the tree seventy yards away pulled down the rifle, stunned by what he had witnessed. What was going on? Someone must have seen him and tipped them off. He scrambled down from the tree and limped back through the woods to his truck.

"Elizabeth, would you excuse Michael and me for a few minutes?" Jay asked once they were inside the front door.

She hesitated, obviously suspicious that whatever was going on concerned her, but she decided to honor his request. Nodding, she turned and climbed the stairs to the bedroom.

Once she was out of earshot, Jay closed the door and withdrew a picture from his jacket pocket. "Remember this guy?"

Michael stared at the glossy black-and-white mug shot of a dark-haired man, heavily bearded, that he vaguely recognized but could not specifically place. "Sort of. Who is he? And what's going on?"

"Tony Laperra. One of the slickest assassins anywhere. You remember his name came up last year in a case? We never could pin anything on him. Apparently he's been stashed away in another country or lying low here. But yesterday I think he showed up in Marietta."

"What?" Michael gasped.

Jay nodded. "He was coming out of a restaurant directly facing your office. It was sheer luck that I recognized him with this heavy beard. Even though he was wearing a baseball cap and casual clothes yesterday, he still has that slight limp from a badly broken leg. And the eyes and nose are the same. I thought it was him, so I tried to follow him but he lost me. I returned to the restaurant and questioned the staff. One of the waitresses said he sat for a long time at a table in a secluded corner. And he was watching your building. I can't be positive, Michael, but all my instincts tell me it was Laperra."

Michael turned grave eyes to Jay, his thoughts racing. "Do you think it's possible—"

"Anything's possible. Remember how the hit-and-run incident at Nick's made front page news? And Elizabeth's name was mentioned. It's quite possible the hit-and-run has left the country; on the other hand, we have to assume he may still be living here as an ordinary citizen. And he may know that Elizabeth can identify him."

Michael chewed his lip thoughtfully. "He could be a prominent man who doesn't want to be identified. That would explain why he's been so careful to cover his tracks." He got out of the kitchen chair and started to pace, his brows drawn together in a tight frown. "So you think it's possible he's hired this guy?" He stopped pacing and glared at the picture.

Jay sighed. "We can't overlook that as a possibility. There's some reason Tony has come out of hiding."

Michael picked up the photograph from the kitchen table, and his eyes took in each feature on the man's face. He tilted his head, trying to imagine Laperra without a beard, perhaps a different hair style. Finally, Michael shook his head. "I don't think I've seen him."

"There's something else you should know."

Michael's eyes darted to his younger brother, respecting his sharp instincts as a detective. He was one of the best.

"What is it?" A sense of dread filled Michael, but he had to know what was going on now. His detective agency, Searchers, specialized in finding missing people. He took pride in his ability to do that. Now more than ever, he had to be the best he had ever been at his profession. It was crucial.

He lowered his voice, glancing toward the hallway. "Our guy on the tractor isn't sure, but Laperra may have passed him this morning."

Michael's heart was hammering in his chest. "Did this guy get a good look at him?"

"No, the driver of the car kept his head turned. But he did get the license number. It's a rental vehicle leased by a Tom Leonard."

"Tony Laperra. They tend to use the same initials."

Michael's thoughts whirled. Jay had come out of the chair and now both were pacing the kitchen floor. Jay walked to the sink, staring out at the grounds. "We've got to get her out of here, Michael. We can't take a chance, even a remote one."

Michael stopped pacing and looked at his brother thoughtfully. "Do you really think it's possible that he's been hired to take out Elizabeth? Or all of us?"

"We don't know what to think," Jay countered, "so in the meantime, let's take no chances."

Michael raked a hand through his hair, his mind flying in all directions. "Elizabeth and I were just talking about going back to Cancún. I was hoping maybe that would spark her memory."

"Hey, that's a good idea," Jay said, "but I'd want to have a couple of agents accompany you. Don't worry—I promise they'll look like innocent tourists."

Michael nodded. "Just keep this from Elizabeth. I don't want her feeling any more pressure. It certainly won't help her memory to clear if she starts to panic." He walked to the phone. "I'll call her doctor and if he says we can leave, then I'll get us a flight out tonight. Have your men ready."

Jay nodded. "I'm glad you agree. I'd already planned to take Katie to Mom's myself. I think we should do that now, regardless of what the doctor says about Elizabeth."

The man drove miles out of the way to prevent passing the Calloway house again. Down winding country roads, through another town, he finally reached the interstate. He mentally congratulated himself on being smart, moving just in time. He assessed his next move carefully as he drove along, always observing the speed limit.

Something was up at the Calloway place. A tip? The guy on the tractor? The auto rental shop? Or was it just a coincidence? His instincts had kept him alive and safe. And now his gut feeling was to stash the rental truck, maybe even head for the airport. But first he'd make a phone call. He'd tell the person on the other end that the price on Elizabeth Calloway had just gone up another hundred grand.

Michael and Elizabeth sat in the first-class section of the big jet, awaiting takeoff from Atlanta on an early morning flight.

Michael checked Elizabeth's seat belt, then his own, as the airline stewardess demonstrated the use of oxygen masks. He had hoped to get a flight out last night, but his best possibility was the early bird out of Atlanta to Dallas. A change of planes would take them to Cancún, where they would arrive in the early afternoon.

Automatically, he glanced back around the crowded plane, casually observing each face in a crowd of strangers. Six rows back, he spotted the two detectives from Jay's department, dressed in tourist garb, both peering into the morning newspapers. No one else resembled Laperra, even with an imagined disguise.

Drawing a sigh of relief, Michael turned his attention to Elizabeth, seated by the window, looking out. As the plane taxied down the runway and lifted slowly into a bright, summer blue sky, Michael felt himself begin to relax for the first time.

Katie had been glad to go to Grandma's house with promises of baking chocolate chip cookies and going fishing. Jay had called Michael as soon as Katie was safely installed with her grandparents. As usual, Elizabeth's mother had been difficult about it, until Elizabeth took the phone.

"Mother, I'm going to Cancún. I'd suggest you fly back to London now and resume your life. Maybe we'll come to visit soon."

Michael had been so proud of the way she had handled the

woman who had always managed to dominate them. But he, too, had put his foot down with Millicent this time. He had no alternative.

The detective who had been spending his days puttering in the sun, pretending to work on broken machinery, was grateful to be seated in the cool living room of Oak Shadows. He would wait here for further instructions.

John Logan spread his arms across the back of the Calloways' sofa and sank deeper into the cushions. He had been assigned to watch the house and grounds, and he had backup at the next farm. Half a dozen men were scanning the area for Laperra.

This felt more like a vacation than work. The refrigerator was well stocked, the house was nicer than his cramped apartment, and he felt at peace as he looked through the long windows to the towering oaks. He could see why the Calloways liked it here.

One thing that had caught his eye was the number of Bibles. There was a huge King James version on the hearth, one of those family heirloom types. A modern translation dominated the coffee table, and he had spotted several copies of the book of Psalms in Elizabeth's office. He wondered about that. Maybe they were used as gifts.

He reached toward the coffee table and picked up the New International Version of the Bible, turning the green leather cover. He hadn't brought anything to read, and there was nothing he wanted to watch on television.

Jay had told him the hand of God had held this family together through so much trauma. Maybe if he read the Bible more, he could find a way to mend the relationship with his ex-wife. He had always admired the Calloway brothers. They had been inviting him to go with them to a small group meeting of Promise Keepers, but he had made excuses not to attend. Maybe he would relent the next time he was invited. He wanted the kind of inner strength they had; they seemed so capable of weathering life's storms.

The phone rang and he jumped up and hurried over to the desk. He caught himself just before he lifted the receiver, and mentally practiced speaking in a deeper voice. On the third ring, he lifted the receiver and delivered a nonchalant hello, hoping he sounded like Michael's father.

"Hello," Michael answered him. "Just checking in. I was about to leave from work, and I wanted to know if there had been any messages."

The detective thought back to their conversation earlier. Before Michael and Elizabeth left the country, he would phone from the plane to check on the situation. Just in case the phone was bugged, the detective was supposed to sound like his father, who had dropped in for a visit.

"No, son," he responded calmly. "No messages. Be careful driving home."

"Thanks." The line clicked.

The detective sighed with relief as he hung up. There was no bug in the receiver, he had already checked, but there had been no opportunity to go over the house without arousing suspicion if anyone watched from the woods. Therefore, they had devised this simple plan. In the morning, an electrical service truck would arrive, but the truck was merely on loan, and the driver would be a detective checking out the house.

His eyes were drawn to the open drapes and he walked over and looked out across the vacant lawn. He touched the holstered gun at his side. His work was never easy.

Returning to the sofa, he sat down and picked up the Bible again, flipping idly through the pages. He noticed several verses highlighted. One verse in particular made him pause. He had noticed that verse done in needlepoint on a chair pillow.

"He who began a good work in you will carry it on to completion."

He liked that. He reached for the pen and pocket notepad he always carried. He made a notation of the chapter and verse. Philippians 1:6.

His eyes felt moist as he thought about his two children who had turned out well, thanks to his Christian wife who had kept them in church. He had missed many of their ball games and school functions while working overtime. Jay had told him to be careful; that Michael's marriage got in trouble when his work took precedence over everything else.

He sat staring into space. The only good things that had come out of his life had been those children and a once-happy marriage. He read the verse again. Was his family his good work in life? If so, he should be trying to perfect it rather than avoid it, as he had in the past.

He got up from the sofa and crossed the room to the desk phone. He was going to do what he had vowed never to do: he was going to call Ann and invite her out to dinner on his first night off. Maybe it wasn't too late to try and start over.

He looked around the Calloway house. Perhaps his staying here was for a deeper reason than he had first believed. If so, he was grateful for the lesson he was learning about the kind of strength it took to keep a family together.

ELEVEN

The sky was a brilliant blue as their plane flew into Cancún. Michael turned to Elizabeth, carefully awaiting her reaction as she stared out the window of the jet.

Michael had tried to keep his hopes up even though she was gazing at the aquamarine water and white sands as though she had never been here. He had promised himself he wouldn't ask if she remembered anything; nor would he show his disappointment if it was obvious that she did not. The important thing was that she was safe now. And Katie was safe.

He dragged his eyes from Elizabeth's profile and pressed his head back into the cushioned seat. He so wanted to hold Elizabeth in his arms and have her respond in kind, as she had when they honeymooned here. But he must not push her. He had promised her doctor he would see that she remained calm, took her medicine, and merely languished in the sun.

He took a deep breath as the plane began its descent into Cancún. Perhaps they would rediscover the joy they had once known together. Since there was nothing he could do about the situation in Atlanta, he would have to trust Jay and the department to do their job. Thank God his brother was on this case, along with a team of top-notch investigators. He took another deep breath and glanced back at Elizabeth.

She was thinner by at least seven, maybe ten, pounds because she had no appetite since the accident. The doctor had assured him her loss of appetite was not due to the medication or anything other than the trauma she had suffered. Her hair was pulled back from her face, secured with a clasp at her neck, accenting the loss of weight even more. Her cheekbones jutted over hollow cheeks, and her skin was still pale, accenting brown eyes and soft, red lips.

She was wearing a denim sundress that flowed out from her tiny waist into a wide circle above her ankles. The red sandals and handbag were a vivid complement to the simple denim.

His eyes drifted over her head to the island of Cancún as they approached the landing strip. But he was not thinking of sand and sea; he was thinking about Elizabeth.

She wore no jewelry except for the tiny gold hoops in her ears. She had not put her wedding ring back on her finger since the nurse removed it at the hospital. When she returned home, he had told her it was in the small black velvet box in her dresser. But she chose not to wear the one-carat diamond she had so proudly displayed during their first trip to Cancún. He recalled how she had held it up to the sun, admiring the sparkle of the diamond....

"We're landing," she said, turning her wide eyes to Michael. She looked almost as excited as Katie at Christmas.

He winked at her, nodded, and looked out the window at the airport as the plane touched down. He tried not to think of the man who might want to harm Elizabeth. He tried not to feel any sense of danger. After all, they had two bodyguards shadowing them at all times.

He turned slightly, letting his eyes move slowly back over the passengers. There were his buddies, the tourists. No hint of recognition had touched their features when they angled their way down the narrow aisle, passing Elizabeth and Michael, in search of their seats. They were now engaged in a lively conversation about some convention they would be attending, speaking loud enough for others to hear—if anyone was curious. The passengers, however, appeared to be too interested in their own plans to pay attention to two loud-mouthed conventioneers. Some gazed out the window, while others gathered up their carry-on bags.

Michael suddenly felt good as the plane ground to a halt. Yes, they would be safe here. He felt sure of it.

Tony Laperra couldn't believe his streak of luck. Even though the man had agreed to up the ante an extra hundred grand, Tony decided to board a plane and leave Atlanta. He couldn't bear the confines of a jail or prison cell; no, he could never go back to that again. Never.

And so his choice had been to run, to grab a plane out of Atlanta before the detectives closed in on him.

Then, to his delighted astonishment, there they were at the airport: the Calloways, hurriedly making their way to the airlines counter. He had ventured close enough to overhear their final destination, then he had swiftly moved on, heading to the magazine shop. He had the information he needed, so there was no reason to linger. He would simply take a later flight to Cancún. It would be much easier there to finish the job.

First he would make that phone call, inform the man that he was still on the job. And when the money was wired to him, it would be quite simple to vanish into Brazil. He knew a special place there, one he liked to visit, and one that would provide a safe haven for him for the next couple of years. He was tired of Atlanta and the South, tired of all the bad memories. Yes, he needed a change, and the money would allow him to live well.

He smiled to himself. He had always been lucky, even though most people considered him skilled at his work, which he was. But so many things in life were sheer luck. For a while, luck seemed to have deserted him, but now it had found him again. This would be his last job. He imagined himself somewhere in the future, living an ordinary life in another country, without having to glance over his shoulder, without having to worry about money or women. He would have plenty of both. His footsteps quickened toward the wall of pay phones as he reached for a quarter to call his employer.

Michael had booked the same hotel where he and Elizabeth had stayed on their honeymoon. He had, however, used another name, as a precaution. He even tried to get the same suite, although that was out of the question, due to short notice. Still, it was an impressive resort that overlooked the beach and the Caribbean. The resort featured a huge swimming pool, tennis courts, and three restaurants.

As they walked through the lobby, Elizabeth stopped and frowned up at him.

"What is it?" he asked.

"I think we should get separate rooms."

He stared at her. He hadn't even thought of booking two rooms; after all, they were married. But his heart sank as he looked into her eyes and realized that to her, he was just a good friend. She was not ready for intimacy.

"All right," he said, trying to take her suggestion in stride. "By the way, my secretary booked the hotel room, so it will be in her husband's name. Just thought I'd let you know that."

She stared at him with something in her eyes that looked like suspicion.

It didn't matter, he told himself, stepping into line for the check-in counter. Her safety was more important than trying to assuage her doubt.

As he approached the desk, he began to wonder if it would

be possible to obtain a second room at the last minute, at such a popular resort.

A desk clerk looked pleasantly at him and asked for his name. "William Duke," he replied, then added, "I think my secretary made a mistake when she booked my reservations. I wanted adjoining bedrooms, but she told me just before I left that she had only booked one. Could you help me out?" he asked, flashing a warm smile, trying to sound light hearted.

The dark eyes of the clerk slipped beyond him to Elizabeth, then back to Michael. "Adjoining rooms?" she asked, staring at him for a moment before checking the large register.

"If possible." Michael took a deep breath, wondering how best to handle the situation. He was certain, at this late date, that if she found an extra room it would be on another floor, and how would that work out? The detectives were staying here as well; if necessary, maybe they would agree to find another place. But Jay wouldn't like that idea, he reminded himself.

"You're in luck, Mr. Duke," the clerk said, after studying her book. "We had a cancellation this morning, and I can give you adjoining rooms; however, the beds are regular, not king size."

That was the least of his worries, Michael thought, giving her a grateful smile. "Thank you. That'll be fine."

He signed the register and accepted keys and directions to the rooms. Then he turned to Elizabeth.

"Okay, we're ready."

She had overheard the conversation and seemed pleased that she would have her own room. As they waited for the elevator, Michael spotted the two detectives sauntering into the hotel, appearing not to recognize him as they continued their nonchalant conversations. They were both wearing floral shirts and khaki shorts with tennis shoes. Neither looked like this was an assignment.

The elevator doors swung open, and Elizabeth stepped ahead of Michael as he gripped their suitcases and followed. He gave her the number of their floor and she punched a button. As the elevator climbed upward, neither spoke. Michael wondered what she was thinking. He wanted to ask her if this hotel held any memories for her, but it was a useless question. Obviously she remembered nothing, and his heart was heavy with sadness. When was this nightmare going to end?

The doors swung open and they stepped into the red-carpeted corridor. He led the way down the wide hallway to their rooms, located at the very end. He unlocked the first door and they peered inside.

The room was nicely furnished with Spanish decor. Red-and-gold drapes and bedspread were a pleasing contrast to the soft tan carpet. At the far end, sliding glass doors opened onto a balcony that commanded a sweeping view of the ocean.

"Oh, this is lovely," she said as he set down her suitcase.

"Glad you like it," he said, checking the bathroom, which was well stocked with thick white towels and plenty of perfumed soaps and small samples of toothpaste and shampoo. He turned back into the bedroom and located the door that would lead into the next bedroom. Better not to open it now. He headed for the outside door.

"Why don't you change into something comfortable," he called over his shoulder, "and we'll go for a walk on the beach before dinner? Or a swim if you feel like it."

"A walk on the beach sounds nice," she replied, rather formally.

He nodded and left the room, closing the door behind him. This was ridiculous! Suddenly she was treating him like a stranger, ignoring the fact that they had spent the past two weeks at Oak Shadows with their daughter, in a home they had redecorated together. But even there, they had stayed in separate bedrooms.

The sense of frustration that kept gnawing at him was turning into an ulcer. Sometimes he wondered if Elizabeth was even making an effort to remember. A terrible thought took form: What if she was subconsciously choosing to stay in this twilight zone of childhood so she could feel safe and protected?

As he unlocked his bedroom, entered, and checked out the surroundings, his fears assailed him. Maybe there was a kind of safeguard at work inside her mind; maybe she was afraid to remember. Was it possible she suspected she was in danger, that if her memory returned, the accident she had witnessed would be too horrible for her mind to contain?

He put a hand to his forehead, trying to shut off the chain of thoughts that could spoil the vacation. Setting down the suitcase, he walked across to open the glass doors and stepped onto the balcony.

He leaned forward, gripping the rail, letting the sea breeze sweep over his face and ruffle his hair. He knew the situation would work itself out in time; he merely had to hang on to his patience. But that was becoming more difficult.

He had prayed for wisdom and felt led to get Elizabeth out of Georgia. Cancún seemed remote and reasonably safe. He hadn't reckoned on this strange barrier remaining between them. Again, he closed his eyes. *God, help us through this. Please.*

"Hello, neighbor," a soft voice called.

He turned to face Elizabeth standing on her balcony next to his, and he couldn't resist smiling at her despite his frustration. This was all so bizarre it was almost comical. Yet he couldn't bring himself to laugh.

She was smiling at him, and her brown eyes twinkled as she turned back to view the ocean. "Isn't this lovely?"

He sighed, studying her profile. "Yes, it is." But he was not thinking of the view; he was thinking of the woman he loved with all his heart and soul. The woman with whom he had reconciled after a painful separation. But now…was he losing her again?

TWELVE

Tony Laperra arrived in Cancún an hour after the Calloways. He was not concerned about their location; he would find out in due time. It would not be that difficult to track them down; furthermore, he liked the challenge. That was part of the game.

With only his carry-on bag, he moved through customs, converted some American dollars to pesos, then headed out of the airport in search of a taxi. He found one, and after a casual conversation with the talkative driver, he learned exactly which buses had delivered to the hotel zone within the past hour. He wrote down the names and considered his choices. He had at least half a dozen to choose from, which should present no problem for him.

He decided to be bold and give a description of his "friends," but the taxi driver had failed to notice them. After all, it was a busy afternoon. He was lucky to have the schedule of the hotel buses. Why press luck, when it was going his way?

He chose a modest hotel, located conveniently near the ones he had written in his notebook. Giving the driver a generous tip, he got out, hooked his carry-on over his shoulder and entered the hotel. He smiled to himself. Some jobs presented little challenge; it appeared this would be one of those, even though he had been discouraged by the blunder at their farm. But this time they were conveniently removed from that farm; they had distanced themselves from the security of their home and the detectives who watched from a distance.

He frowned. Was it possible that a detective or two had

tagged along? He'd better check that out. This time there was no margin for error.

Michael and Elizabeth walked along the beach together, hand in hand. They both wore shorts and T-shirts and tennis shoes, and as he held her hand, Michael began to relax. She seemed to be warming up to him again, and he thanked God for small favors.

"Elizabeth, do you remember how we sat on this beach—" he stopped walking and leaned down—"and you said the sand looked like talcum powder?" He scooped up a handful and let it drift through his fingers.

She knelt beside him, gathering a handful, pressing it between her fingers. Her eyes slowly moved up to his face, and he thought he saw a glimmer of recognition in her eyes.

"I remember the feel of it," she said, turning back to the sand, running her hand along its surface. "It looks like talcum powder and yet it's firm," she said, fascinated. She picked up another handful and, like Michael, let it sift through her fingers and filter to the ground. "Oh Michael, I know we were happy here. I'm happy now."

"Good," he said as they stood and he slipped his arm around her shoulders. "I want you to enjoy yourself. I want you to have a good time and relax. Don't try to force your mind to remember. It will come back naturally."

His words sounded more confident than he felt, but at least she had given him a ray of hope. He could cling to that.

Other tourists strolled the beach, played in the water, or simply lay on towels or reclined in beach chairs, soaking up the brilliant sun. Although it was ninety degrees, the coolness of the water offset the heat as Michael and Elizabeth walked toward the water's edge.

"Want to take off our shoes and wade into the water?"

He remembered she had enjoyed that before, and he had followed her then, feeling a bit silly. It was his style to dive right in, but she was a wader, and he had gone along with her until—

"Do you remember when we were wading along this shoreline and I got mean and ducked you?" he teased her, as they stood together, watching the gentle waves lap toward shore.

Her eyebrow lifted in surprise. Then a grin played over her mouth. "Would you really do that?"

Suddenly, as they stood there gazing into one another's eyes, he felt himself falling in love with her all over again. Maybe that would happen for her; maybe for a short while there could be another honeymoon after the past torturous weeks.

"You bet. And once you get your bathing suit on, I may be unable to resist the temptation to do it again." He winked.

She merely laughed, turning back from the water. Obviously, she didn't want to go wading, fearing that his playfulness might overpower his good intentions.

"It feels so good to walk like this," she said, drawing a deep breath of the fresh invigorating breeze. "And with you," she added, reaching for his hand again.

He looked down at her and fought an impulse to place a kiss on her lips. "It feels good for me, too. I've been working too hard."

She nodded. "For me."

He did not deny that, for she would know it was a lie, and it was very important for her to trust him. He merely shrugged and pointed out to the horizon. "See the sailboat?"

Elizabeth nodded. The boat bobbed lazily along, drifting aimlessly with the water.

"Yes, it must feel so…carefree to do that," she said, staring out at the boat.

"Maybe we'll rent a sailboat while we're here," he said, angling a glance down at her, hoping to spark a memory.

She did not respond; she just continued to watch the sailboat with a vague smile. He knew she did not remember their day of sailing. *Give her time,* he told himself, for he was beginning to see a little bit of progress with her.

After a dozen phone calls, Laperra had failed to locate them, and then a realization struck him. Calloway had not registered under his own name. He frowned at that, hung up the phone, and shoved his hands in the pockets of his Bermuda shorts. He had been foolish even to think he would.

He strolled across the room and stepped out on the balcony.

His eyes swept the beach, noting the many tourists. Did his anonymous registration mean that Calloway merely wanted privacy, or was he aware they were being stalked?

He didn't like that idea at all. The breeze wafted over him, calming his nerves. He needed a Scotch and a dip in the ocean. Turning back into his room and scooping his keys from the dresser, he reminded himself of an important issue: Calloway was off his home turf. They were in another country. There was a limit to how many bodyguards he could bring, and besides that, Calloway probably assumed they were safe.

He checked the lock on the door, stepped into the corridor, closed the door behind him, and headed for the bar.

Michael and Elizabeth had decided on the seafood buffet offered by the hotel. Now, at a small, candlelit table, they feasted on fresh boiled shrimp with a luscious salad and homemade bread.

126

"Oh Michael, this is so wonderful." Elizabeth smiled across the candlelight.

She was wearing a white sundress, and her golden hair was parted on the side and flowed to her shoulders. She looked relaxed and happy for the first time, and Michael noticed that her appetite was perking up. He ordered another basket of bread, recalling how much she had liked it before.

"The taste of things," she said, glancing at their plates. "I'm remembering something spicy here."

"The cocktail sauce for the shrimp. It was too strong for you before, and we had to order a milder type."

The glow in her brown eyes dimmed as she shook her head slowly, swirling her hair lightly around her shoulders. "Isn't it disgusting that I could remember something so trivial and not—" she broke off, hating to voice the words.

There was no point in saying what Michael knew. *And not remember my husband!*

"It will come back to you, Elizabeth. I must remind you, the doctor told us that we have to build our way back, and often a person starts with simple little flashes—smells, tastes, the feel of something."

She reached across the table and grasped his hand. "I do remember the feel of your hands," she said, her eyes softening. "That came back to me today, walking the beach. The strength, the gentleness you possess...."

Their eyes locked over the candlelight and Michael's heart beat faster. With all of his heart, he hoped and prayed that their relationship could be as it had been before. They had been through so much and yet they had held on. It would be so wonderful to start over here. Now.

Someone passed their table, and he glimpsed one of the detectives heading enthusiastically for the huge buffet table.

He dropped his eyes. He didn't want Elizabeth to see the disappointment there; the sight of the detective was a reminder that her life was still in danger and would be until Jay tracked down the killer.

"Well," he said, glancing toward the dessert bar, "how's your sweet tooth tonight?"

She laughed. "My sweet tooth."

He nodded. "Lucky you, never one for sweets, but there's a piece of Key lime pie over there calling my name."

She laughed. "Then let's have Key lime pie."

They got up and walked toward the dessert bar. Michael was not about to tell her she had never liked Key lime pie.

"What do you mean you haven't found them?" the man in Atlanta growled into the telephone. "This is your second day there. Her memory could come back any time. Your expense account doesn't include sleeping on the job."

"I wouldn't call four hours a decent night's sleep," Laperra retaliated.

"Look, get on it first thing. You're smart; you can find them. Look in the obvious places, the ritzy hotels and—"

"Don't tell me how to do my job!" Laperra rallied back. "I'm going to try a different plan today. I think it'll work."

"I don't want to know about it. I just want the results," the man snapped and slammed down the phone.

He called his office and informed his administrative assistant that he had come down with a virus and wouldn't be in today. Cutting off her reminder of his schedule, he sharpened his tone and told her to cancel everything.

"Karen, my physician ordered bed rest until this thing clears up. You can handle things for me, I'm confident of that. Now I really must hang up."

She offered a sympathetic comment just before he replaced the phone. He stood up, then gripped the edge of the desk, feeling shaky. His addiction was consuming him now; with tension eating away his insides, he could no longer confine his habit to evening. Lately it had taken a small dose upon arising, then an extra pot of coffee. Today, however, both had failed to calm him.

With a quick glance at the door to assure himself it was locked, he walked to the picture and slid it back, inserting the key into the lock of the safe. Diving into the front of the safe, he retrieved the bag of white powder, noting he was getting low. He couldn't worry about that now; he'd call his supplier. He had to have relief.

The illness he felt was worse than a virus, much worse. But it was too late to stop it.

THIRTEEN

Katie had enjoyed spending Sunday with Grandma and Grandpa and Jay and Tracy. She had spent the past hour playing outside with Sam, the collie, but then she started feeling homesick and went back in the house to see what everyone was doing.

They were gathered in the den, with Jay and Tracy on the sofa, Grandpa Mike in his recliner, Grandma in her matching one. They were not smiling, as they had at the lunch table; instead, they were talking in the low voices adults use when they are trying to keep a secret.

"Not a word. Nothing," Jay said, frowning.

She was smart enough to know that something was going on, but she wasn't exactly sure what it was. Then suddenly Grandma turned and saw her and a quick smile broke over her face.

"Come in, darling. Come join us."

"Why don't you bring us some of those good cookies you and Grandma made last night?" Grandpa Mike yelled.

Katie hesitated. Since she had been here, all they did was eat. She hated to tell them, but she was beginning to get a stomachache from so much food. She could see why Grandma and Grandpa complained of being overweight.

"I'm not hungry," she replied, walking toward Tracy. "Are you?"

Tracy rubbed her stomach. "Not after eating so much fried chicken and creamed potatoes."

Katie looked at Jay. "What about you?"

Jay stretched his feet out before him and sank deeper into

the sofa. "I can't hold another crumb, Katie." He turned and looked affectionately at his father. "Dad, we're all stuffed!"

Jay reached for Katie's hand, pulling her over to sit between him and Tracy. "For as long as I can remember, your grandpa has worried about his family having enough good food, and that has *never* been a problem in this house."

"It's because you and Michael were in sports," Grandma spoke up. "We felt you needed an extra portion to build muscles, and I guess we just never got out of the habit. I still cook for a crowd, even when there's only Mike and me here to eat."

"That's because we usually had a crowd when the boys were growing up," Grandpa chuckled.

Katie looked across at her grandfather, relieved to see him more relaxed today. He had acted like he didn't feel good when he came to her house, but now, back home, he seemed to feel better. She was glad.

"You know, Katie, I'm counting on you to be my little helper when the baby comes," Tracy said, giving Katie a hug.

Katie turned to her, interested in the conversation for the first time. "I'm excited about the baby."

"Only six more weeks," Jay said, looking across at his father. "Are you ready for a grandson, Dad?"

Katie looked at her grandpa. When he was proud of someone, his chest seemed to expand half a size bigger. "You bet!"

"Are you ready for a granddaughter?" Tracy asked Grandma.

Everyone laughed.

"Katie, we don't know if we're having a boy or a girl. We want it to be a surprise," Tracy explained.

"Wish I'd been able to know the outcome when you guys were born," Grandma laughed. "But I'm glad we had two boys," she said, glancing at Grandpa with a warm look in her eyes.

Katie stared at Tracy's stomach. She wondered how she could carry so much weight around.

Tracy jumped. "Oops!" Then she grabbed Katie's hand. "Want to feel the baby kick?"

Katie let Tracy guide her hand to the smooth shirt covering her stomach. Beneath her fingers she could feel a light thump. That was her cousin!

She giggled, holding her hand very still, waiting for another kick. But the baby had decided to be still.

"He always does that," Jay laughed. "Whenever anyone wants him to do one thing, he does the other."

"Or *she*," Tracy corrected him.

The phone rang and everyone jumped. Katie frowned, wondering why a ringing phone made them all so nervous.

"I'll get it," Grandma said, hurriedly getting up from her recliner.

Everyone was silent, waiting to hear who was calling. Then as soon as Grandma said hello, she began to motion to Katie. "Hello, Michael. How are you two doing? Good, glad to hear it. That's good, too. Here's Katie."

Katie took the phone. "Hi, Dad."

"Hey, honey!" The sound of his voice made her miss her daddy, and she felt more homesick than ever for Oak Shadows.

"When are you coming home?" she blurted.

"In a few days. You're having a good time, aren't you?"

She nodded. "I caught more fish than Grandpa."

"Good girl. Hey, wanna speak to Mom?"

"Sure!"

She could hear a low murmur and then her mother spoke up. "Hello, Katie. How are you?"

Katie frowned. Something in her mother's tone was different. Not different, really; it was the same way she talked ever

133

since she came home from the hospital. Katie just wished she'd be more friendly with her. She wanted them to be the way they were before the accident.

"I'm having a good time," Katie said, knowing that was what everyone wanted her to say. "Are you having fun, Mom?" she asked in a cautious voice.

"Yes, a lot of fun. We'll see you soon."

Katie frowned. That wasn't much of a conversation. Then her dad came back on, told her the beach was nice, and they'd all go to Florida later in the summer. But she wasn't really listening. She was still thinking about her mother, still wondering about the funny tone in her voice.

She handed the phone back to her grandmother with a sigh, then looked across at Jay and Tracy. "I guess Mom doesn't have her strength back yet."

He had been the first customer at the marina that morning, so there was no problem in renting a small boat. His instincts told him the couple would probably walk the beach early, before the heat became intense, and this way he could spot them.

With his binoculars and a tiny camera tucked in his pocket, he had climbed into the boat and was now drifting away from the marina out into the emerald water. Through his tinted sunglasses, he gazed at the horizon, blurred by the unrelenting blueness of the clean sky. A cooling breeze wafted over him, calming his nerves. He had made the foolish mistake of consuming too much Scotch the night before. He tried not to drink on the job, but he enjoyed his Scotch, and the temptation for more than one belt had seized him. He had paid for his indulgence with a slight headache when his wake-up call came at six. He vowed not to be careless again; he needed steady hands and a clear mind for the task at hand.

Now the feel of wind and water invigorated him, restoring the oxygen to his brain, and he was ready to do the job. In fact, he hoped to get it over with today. He didn't particularly like Cancún; he preferred a more remote place, something less touristy. And yet, the tourists worked to his advantage.

He lifted his wrist to check his Rolex. Nine o'clock. Calloway was an early riser, he knew that much. The woman probably slept later. Nevertheless, they should be up and about by now. He positioned the boat seat to where he could focus on the shoreline as he traveled at a slow speed. From his pockets, he removed his binoculars and began to scan the shore.

All shapes and sizes appeared in the lenses. He knew how to be patient; it was essential in his line of work. He cruised on, concentrating on the private beaches of the luxury hotels. Once he thought he spotted a woman resembling Elizabeth Calloway, but her male companion was blonde as well, and he doubted Michael would resort to bleaching his hair. That was not his style.

He cruised on. An hour later, his venture paid off. A couple wearing bathing suits were wading in the water along the shoreline at one of the most elite hotels. He let the boat idle and focused his lenses.

He gazed at the couple frolicking in the water for several seconds, and a slow, confident grin worked at his hard mouth.

No mistake. He had found them!

Carefully, he laid the binoculars on his lap and reached for the camera. He took several shots of them, wanting to capture the exact way they looked here, now. He needed the pictures as proof that he had the right people, and these would be given to his employer. And more importantly, he had vital information for himself. He knew where they were staying. Now it would just be a matter of time until he cornered them.

~~~~~

"Michael," Elizabeth said, reaching for his hand, "I love feeling the cool water lap over my toes."

"You always have," he said, embracing her lightly.

She was warming up to him now, and this pleased him. Often she was making the first move, reaching for his hand, or touching his shoulders, and he read a different look in her eyes when they rested on him. The confusion was giving way to something else, something he recognized as love.

Thank you, God, he silently prayed. Whether she remembered everything clearly was suddenly not important. The fact that she, too, was falling in love all over again warmed his heart and almost brought tears of gratitude to his blue eyes.

"Want to go for a swim?" he asked after they had played in the water for several minutes. "The pool is not crowded, and I think we'd enjoy lounging around there."

"Yes, let's." She beamed up at him.

Holding hands, they walked back toward the hotel.

Elizabeth felt a rush of happiness each time she looked into Michael's face. She knew she had loved this man before, for she was falling in love with him now. She could see why she had chosen to marry him, to be the mother of his child. He was so kind and considerate, so understanding. And she had not seen a man anywhere who appealed to her the way this one did. She stopped walking as a memory rushed back. "You like deep-sea fishing. I remember...."

"What?" he said, excited. "What do you remember?"

She closed her eyes, trying to recapture the image.

"You were standing on..." She snapped her fingers repeatedly. "You were standing on some kind of platform with a fishing

136

pole in one hand and a huge fish in the other. *I remember that, Michael! It was you!*"

He pulled her against his chest, hugging her hard. "It was our best day here. You insisted that we go out deep-sea fishing because you knew I wanted to do that. You were a great sport, even though you got a little seasick. I caught a huge marlin, then nearly lost him. When finally we were back at the marina, you took pictures of me. The reason that memory is so sharp is because you were so excited snapping pictures that you backed off the dock and fell into the water!"

They were both laughing now. "The pictures didn't turn out," Michael said.

"And I think I ruined the camera," she laughed.

Michael felt as if his heart were bursting. Her memory was coming back to her slowly, but now he was confident it would. She was identifying the things that stood out sharply in her mind.

"What about the hotel?" he said as they climbed the steps back up to the sprawl of the huge pool and lawn area.

She nodded. "It's becoming familiar to me. The cool water of the pool, the feel of your hands steadying me." She paused and looked into his face and their eyes locked.

Michael saw it now, the feelings she was still hesitant to verbalize. She had mentioned the strength and the gentleness in his hands last night and then they had said good night and he had gone to his bedroom to sleep alone. He suspected she was remembering more. Maybe tonight would be different.

"Okay, last one in the pool gets ducked," he said, his happiness bursting into an exuberant shout.

"That'll be you," she said, diving in before he had finished his sentence.

They had laughed and frolicked and then climbed out of the pool and headed for the towel station, where an attendant handed them long beach towels.

Elizabeth ruffled her hair with the towel, then combed it back from her face with her hands. Although her face was still thin, Michael noticed that the sun was bringing a glow to her skin, and for the first time since the accident she was beginning to look healthy again.

Returning the used towels, they were given fresh ones to fold around them. They followed the stone walkway around to the elevator and proceeded up to the fifth floor.

"Would you prefer to go someplace else for lunch?" Michael asked as the elevator opened and they headed toward their rooms. This time he unlocked her bedroom and entered with her, unlatching the door to his adjoining room. "You know, there are lots of wonderful restaurants here. I have a suggestion. Since we ate a hearty breakfast, why don't we have a light lunch and go shopping? I think you're going to remember that special store where you found more jewelry than I could afford to buy you at the time. You said the prices were great, and the jewelry was quality stuff. Want to go back?"

"Sure," she smiled, totally agreeable.

"Okay," Michael said, lingering for a moment longer. "I'll get ready." He turned and went into his bedroom, through the adjoining door, not bothering to close it. Neither did she. He smiled. *We're making progress.*

As they walked through the lobby, an afternoon crowd had gathered in one of the restaurants. A woman's voice floated to them. It was a beautiful voice that sang a hauntingly familiar refrain, one that shook Michael to the core. He studied

Elizabeth's profile. She seemed strangely fascinated by the song.

"Want to step inside and listen?" he asked.

She nodded and they walked to the door. It was a long room with tables arranged in a circular fashion. The room was crowded, but the people were silent, listening intently to the singer. She was young, in her twenties, but her voice was strong and she gave a lovely rendition of an old song. The song was especially meaningful to Michael now, and he had to fight his emotions as he listened. Elizabeth looked fascinated, as well.

It was a song they had both loved. The young woman stood beside the piano, holding the microphone, singing softly yet poignantly, and the message in the song captured both Michael and Elizabeth:

Memories…light the corners of my mind.
Misty, watercolor memories…of the way we were.

Elizabeth looked up at Michael, her eyes shining, and he put his arm around her, holding her close against his chest as they listened:

Can it be that it was all so simple then,
Or has time rewritten every line?
If we had the chance to do it all again,
Tell me would we? Could we?

"Michael, that's so beautiful," she whispered.

He nodded, unable to say anything.

So it's the laughter that we'll remember.
Whenever we remember the way we were.

Her voice drifted into the silence, then suddenly a round of applause filled the room, with shouts of, "*MORE!*"

Memories…light the corners of my mind.
Misty, watercolor memories…of the way we were.

With the love song floating in the background, Elizabeth

turned to Michael, her eyes filling with tears.

"Michael, I love you. Maybe I don't remember much about my life before the accident, but I know that I loved you then, and I love you now."

Michael pulled her into his arms, not caring that they were standing in a busy hotel in Cancún. A memory had come back to her, a memory of their love. In time, all the memories would come back, the amnesia would clear.

He kissed her lips and smoothed her hair back from her face. "It's going to be okay, Elizabeth. God has given us a love that will see us through the hardships. We're going to make it."

And he felt that they would. Despite a killer stalking them and danger lurking in the background, they would make it.

"Elizabeth, after you there was never anyone else. Even in my thoughts. No other woman has had any appeal."

She looked into his eyes and smiled. "You loved me that much?"

"I love you even more now." He looked around. "People are staring at us," he said under his breath. "Come on."

Hand in hand, they strolled out the door to the restaurant nearby, where they had first dined.

"We've been here," she said as they entered the huge restaurant.

"Yes, we have. Our first big dinner when we honeymooned here."

Happiness flowed through Michael now, a clean, refreshing love that soothed away the dark clouds, like a gentle rain after a storm.

The hostess seated them in a cozy booth where they feasted on a seafood salad, then set off on their shopping trip. Michael had decided against taking a bus, even though it had been fun riding the buses before and observing the local people. The buses were crowded, and Michael thought it unwise to expose themselves to strangers, even though he had glimpsed the detectives out for their daily walk as he and Elizabeth left the hotel.

He flagged down a taxi and they jumped in. Michael announced the name of the store where they were going. Once they were in the backseat, the taxi roared off.

"It occurs to me that you must be very prosperous in your profession. Does your agency, Searchers, provide a good salary?"

"It does. And you have a good practice as a Christian psychologist." He leaned back against the cushions and smiled at her. "In the area of finances, we're doing just fine."

"I keep trying to imagine myself counseling people, trying to help them—"

"You do help them, Elizabeth. You've helped a lot of people. You're devoted to your work, just as I am. That caused us some problems for a while, but not anymore." He squeezed her hand as he spoke.

She nodded, taking in everything he had told her as she turned back to the window.

The store was located several miles from their hotel, and this gave them an opportunity to study other luxurious hotels along the way.

"I like where we're staying," Elizabeth said, snuggling against his shoulder. "We loved that hotel, didn't we?"

"Yes, we did." He nuzzled his cheek against her hair, absorbing the smell of sunshine and the shampoo she used. Hot air drifted through an open window. The early-morning weather report had predicted that the temperature would climb to ninety degrees again, and the humidity intensified once they were away from the ocean breeze. Both were perspiring by the time the taxi swerved to the curb of the store they were seeking.

The window of the store advertised handcrafted items, clothing, and jewelry, and as they entered the air-conditioned building, they breathed a sigh of relief.

Elizabeth looked around and nodded. "This is impressive. There seems to be everything here. Where do we start?"

Michael shrugged. "Depends on if you want clothing, leather goods, or gold and silver. The last time we were here, you expressed a preference for the silver jewelry."

Elizabeth's eyes slipped over the shop. "Silver jewelry. Yes." She whirled to him. "Did I buy a silver charm bracelet?"

Michael grinned from ear to ear. "You certainly did. And we added a charm with each memorable event in our life. It's at home in your drawer."

Her eyes twinkled as though she had just discovered a special prize, and she had: a wonderful memory tucked away in the depths of her mind.

They walked in the direction of the silver jewelry and Elizabeth looked delighted by the variety of items.

"Our budget has improved since our last trip here," Michael said, "so this time you don't have to haggle over prices. Get whatever appeals to you. We're here to have a good time."

They reached a glass display case, and an eager young salesman rushed to greet them.

"May I be of service?"

Michael nodded. "Perhaps. The lady would like to see something." He looked at Elizabeth. "What will it be?"

"Rings," she said. "And I would like to take something back to Katie."

"What about Tracy?" Michael asked without thinking.

Her eyes were blank.

"Tracy is Jay's wife."

"Jay?"

"My brother. They came to the hospital when you were very ill, and Tracy stayed with me half the night. She called your mother in London and helped me out in other ways."

Elizabeth dropped her eyes, as though embarrassed. "I'll probably know her when I see her."

"You saw her in the hospital, honey, and you didn't know her. But you were still groggy. Maybe when you see her again…"

The man was bringing out a tray of silver rings, gleaming against their navy velvet background.

"Here is a nice one." He selected one and offered it to Elizabeth. "This is a sterling silver ring with a garnet cluster stone and marcasite set around the center stone."

"Do you like it?" Michael asked.

"Oh yes," Elizabeth beamed, slipping it on her right hand. It fit perfectly.

"Want it?"

Elizabeth looked at him and nodded.

"Okay, now let's pick out something for Katie." He turned back to the man. "Can you find something suitable for an eight-year-old girl?"

"Of course." He turned and walked to the end of the counter and retrieved an object from its case. "This is a favorite of younger people. It's a silver chain with a sterling silver calendar coin."

Elizabeth lifted the coin pendant and nodded. "It might be a little old for her, but it would be a nice keepsake."

"I chose the smallest size," the salesman volunteered.

"Then we'll take it," Michael said. "Now what about Tracy?"

Elizabeth frowned. "I don't know what her tastes are."

143

Michael sighed, wondering about that himself. After looking at several rings, they decided on a bracelet with amber stones.

"I think anyone would like that one," Elizabeth said, studying the bracelet.

Michael nodded. "Come to think of it, I've noticed that she wears bracelets quite often." He looked back at the salesman, who was hovering anxiously. "Wrap them all up and give me the total." He winked at Elizabeth. "I just hope I brought enough money."

He remembered Elizabeth raving about how she could buy quality silver here for half of what she would pay at home, so he wasn't worried. But now Elizabeth was looking concerned and Michael touched her arm reassuringly. "Just teasing."

He paid the bill and Elizabeth watched with interest as the man carefully wrapped each item in tissue.

"I want to wear my ring," she said before he could wrap it.

The man smiled and started to hand it to her, then hesitated and placed the ring in Michael's palm.

Michael carefully placed the ring on her finger, pleased by her approving smile.

"You know," he said gently, "you have a very pretty ring in your jewelry box at home. I'd like to see it on your finger again."

She nodded. "The wedding ring you gave me."

He smiled. He'd wanted to ask; now he finally had the nerve. "Why don't you wear it, Elizabeth?"

She reached for his hand and lifted it to her lips. "Because I didn't feel married to you until we came here. Now I know that I am. I'll put the ring on my finger as soon as we go home."

That statement filled his heart with joy, and he wanted to grab her and kiss her passionately. But then he realized they were standing in the middle of a store, and it would only embarrass Elizabeth for him to show so much emotion.

They left the store, arm in arm, and headed down the sidewalk.

"Oh Michael, look!" Elizabeth pointed.

There were numerous stalls of jewelry and handmade items with vendors hawking their wares.

"Come see what we have," one beckoned. "There's a silver necklace made just for you, señorita!"

Elizabeth laughed and glanced at Michael.

"The last time we were here," he whispered, "you said you didn't want any of those items."

She shrugged lightly. "I'd still like to look."

"Whatever you say."

Michael was feeling good about the way things were going. In fact, he was more lighthearted than he had been since the accident. It was as though they had magically left their troubles behind in the States and were rediscovering the pleasure of a vacation away from problems and worries. And, best of all, Elizabeth was beginning to treat him like a husband again.

They turned into the strip of booths, moving casually from one to another. It was early afternoon and the tourist crowd was out in full force, crowding the booths, forcing them to move at a slower pace.

Suddenly, someone bumped his arm. On guard, he whirled and saw the detective dressed like a tourist, but his nonchalant manner was gone. His face held an intense expression as Michael met his eye.

"Excuse me," he said, looking meaningfully at Michael then pointedly staring into the distance behind Elizabeth.

All of Michael's defenses lunged to the surface as he reached for Elizabeth while turning to follow the man's gaze across the crowded shops. He spotted the other detective at a jewelry booth almost twenty yards away. If Laperra was here, the other detective had him in sight, and this was Michael's warning.

"What's wrong?" Elizabeth was looking up at him curiously.

"It's very crowded; stay close to me," he said in a voice that he hoped did not betray his anxiety.

His eyes inched over every strange face. The detective who had issued the warning moved on, heading directly toward the jewelry booth where his partner waited.

"Let's take a look over here." Elizabeth was pointing to a display of pewter at the adjoining stall.

"Okay," Michael answered absently, his eyes never leaving the detectives. The one standing at the booth had turned to peer around the far side of the aisle, a row that ran parallel to theirs but was blocked from Michael's vision by the stalls.

Laperra must be in that row somewhere, Michael thought. His eyes darted around the jumbled stalls, trying to find the safest place to direct Elizabeth. A quick sweep of the crowd revealed that the main entrance by the public sidewalk was the safest route. They would have a better chance of getting away by taking that way.

Michael kept one eye on the crowd around them, the other on the detectives as he stayed beside Elizabeth, his arm around her shoulder. He tried not to think about the possibility of Laperra so close to them; maybe the detectives were mistaken. How could he have found them?

Those thoughts raced through his mind while he attempted to make the right decision. As much as he wanted to catch Laperra, he had to put Elizabeth's safety first. He had to get her out of here.

"Why don't we go, Elizabeth?" he asked casually. "I'm feeling claustrophobic in here."

"Are you serious?" she asked, tilting her face up to him.

"Yes, I am. Let's head toward the front."

"Okay. I don't see anything anyway."

She slipped her hand in his, interpreting his closeness to her as something to do with his complaint of claustrophobia. He guided her along the far edge of the stalls, keeping as much distance as possible between them and the area where the detectives had spotted somebody, maybe Laperra. He tried to formulate a plan. He could leave the task of capturing Laperra to them; but in his heart, he knew he could probably flush him out better. If they had him in range, they couldn't let him get away! There wouldn't be a better opportunity.

A group of senior citizens had just disembarked from a tourist bus and were making a dash down the aisle of stalls. A heavyset woman led the way, marching determinedly toward them, momentarily cutting off the path he had chosen.

Turning his back to the detectives, hoping to shield Elizabeth in case Laperra came from another direction, he put both hands on her shoulders. Carefully, he guided her past the tour group.

In the next instant, his name was being shouted above the other voices rising and falling in conversation. Before he could turn around, he and Elizabeth were shoved to the dirty concrete. Elizabeth cried out as she fell, but Michael managed to cushion her head against his chest.

Suddenly, one detective knelt beside them while the other struggled with a man who had just dropped a switchblade.

Michael's breath caught in his throat as his eyes met Tony Laperra's evil glare. In that fleeting glimpse, Michael studied the bold features, crooked nose, and hard mouth and knew there was no mistaking this man.

In the next instant, Laperra threw the detective over his

shoulder into a display of china. Dishes clattered and broke as the crowd scattered, yelling, staring from a distance in morbid fascination.

"He's getting away," the detective who was holding onto Elizabeth shouted at Michael.

"Stay with her," Michael said, leaping to his feet. Michael knew he had a better chance of catching Laperra than the other detective, who had scrambled to his feet and taken off after him. The other man was older and slightly heavier than Michael.

Michael tried to bypass the crowd, but he collided head-on with a senior citizen who was yelling about rude people. Faces were a blur as Michael struggled to get past the excited crowd and reach the sidewalk to chase Laperra. Something crashed behind him. An American tourist was yelling for the police, while excited voices joined in Spanish.

A cold sweat broke over him as he reached the sidewalk, gasping for air. The other detective was halfway down the block, darting from one side to another as pedestrians jumped out of his way, staring after him.

Michael bolted after the detective, staring through the maze of people and shops in search of Laperra. In the next block, he spotted a tall, dark-haired man shoving his way through the crowd. A woman fell to the ground, yelling after him.

Michael quickened his pace, his stomach knotting, his blood racing. Dodging, colliding, pressing on, he caught up with the first detective.

The man was already short-winded, and as he glimpsed Michael beside him, the look of surprise turned to relief as he jabbed the air with his finger, pointing toward Laperra in the next block.

Michael picked up speed, apologizing in his haste as he

bumped a young woman. He stepped off the curb into the edge of the street and narrowly missed being hit by a car. The screech of brakes and blare of a horn followed him.

As he reached the next block his subject came into range. Tall, moving with a limp, Laperra was an easy target to follow through the masses of people.

Laperra reached the corner and turned down a side street, cutting off Michael's view of him. Michael stretched his legs to catch up, jumping back onto the sidewalk just as a tour bus dodged him. He could hear the excited shrieks of the people on the bus as he frantically raced down the block. Perspiration poured down his face, and his heart pounded wildly in his chest. He tried to pace himself while stretching every muscle for all he was worth.

Ahead, the light changed and traffic stopped. The crowd came to a halt, and again Michael was forced to leap into the street to keep from crashing into the waiting pedestrians. At the end of the block, he turned down the side street after Laperra. Perspiration dripped from his forehead, stinging his eyes. He blinked, staring straight ahead. Laperra was nowhere in sight!

He slowed down, looking right to left, the shops blurring on each side of him. He searched for a side street, an alley, someplace that could provide an escape route, but there was nothing.

He stopped running, pressing his hand to his chest where his heart was begging for relief. His eyes scanned the shops in front of him, behind him, across the street.

Laperra had cut into one of these shops, but which one?

Michael chose the largest shop on the block, reacting more from instinct than reason. Once inside, he lunged headlong into a rack of women's dresses, sending the display crashing to the floor.

His knees buckled and in the next instant he was on the floor, surrounded by colorful skirts. An irate salesclerk stood above him, talking half in Spanish, half in English, voicing her outrage.

He jumped up from the floor, shoving his hands into his pockets and thrusting a wad of bills into her hand. Quickly he scanned the shop, catching a brief glimpse of surprised faces staring in his direction, but Laperra was not here.

How could I have lost him? Michael closed his eyes as a sick dizziness swept over him. *I was so close!*

He ran back toward the street, looking up and down. He began to open and close shop doors, peering inside. He turned back toward the street, hating himself for letting Laperra get away.

There was nothing left to do but return to Elizabeth, be sure that she was okay. He rushed up the street and met the other detective, looking frazzled from the chase.

Michael shook his head. "He got away."

The detective swore under his breath, placing his hands on his hips, swiveling his head from side to side, as though he might come up with an alternate plan.

"Stay here and watch, just in case he comes out of a shop somewhere. I'm going back to check on Elizabeth."

The detective nodded as Michael rushed back toward the open-air market.

Ahead, he could see a mob gathered at the entrance, and a police car was parked out front. He began to run, his concern for Elizabeth mounting. Once he reached the market, he saw the detective talking with the police, his arm around Elizabeth.

Michael rushed to her side, taking her in his arms. "Come on, honey."

The detective paused in his flow of conversation to the

attentive police. "Yes, get her out of here," he said to Michael.

Michael took Elizabeth's arm and steered her quickly from the crowd, back onto the sidewalk, flagging down a taxi.

"Where are we going?" she asked, looking dazed.

"Honey, I think we'd better go home."

"Home to Oak Shadows?" she asked. One side of her cheek was red from the fall she had taken, and her hair was mussed.

He reached up to smooth her hair. He nodded an answer. "It isn't safe here."

Elizabeth clutched his arm, and when Michael looked at her, her face was deathly pale. She began to tremble.

"Michael," she said in a weak voice, "I'm afraid."

"It's okay now," he said, pulling her gently against his chest as a taxi swerved to the curb.

"No," she said, her voice muffled against his shirt. "It's just beginning. The fear, I mean. And the shock. I'm starting to remember what happened."

Michael was so intent on getting them into the backseat of the taxi that it took a few moments for her words to register. Then suddenly he tilted her cheek and looked into her brown eyes. The pupils were dilated with emotion.

"It's all coming back to me." She dropped her face into her hands. "And it's terrible."

FOURTEEN

Once they were back in the safety of the hotel room, Elizabeth sat with Michael and the two detectives.

"I don't know if it was the fright or the fall or what, but my head has cleared."

"Tell us about the night of the accident," one of the detectives gently prompted.

Her brown eyes widened in her pale face as she stared into the distance. "I know that I was meeting Michael that night and—"

She frowned, turning to look out at the tranquil ocean.

"And what?" Michael asked gently.

"I remember the feel of the soft summer breeze on my face. A car was pulling out of a parking space somewhere behind me," she said, her voice a monotone. She seemed completely lost in the memory. "A woman and a child. And then...another car whipped around the corner of the building." She hesitated, looking desperately at Michael. "I got out and ran toward the car...I had to try and stop him...he was going to hit the other car...."

"Take it easy, honey." He gripped her hand. "Just tell us what you saw."

She blinked, staring into space. "It was a black car, a sports model, and the man..." She closed her eyes for a moment, trying to recall every detail of the horrid scene. Then she opened her eyes and shook her head. "I knew him, but I can't think who he was. But Michael, I believe it will come to me," she said, squeezing his hand.

"This is wonderful." He looked back at the detectives. "But

Laperra is still the link to this other man. We have to find him."

"Where do we look?" one asked.

Michael stared out at the ocean, trying to put himself in Laperra's shoes. "Either he'll lie low, or he'll get off the island as quickly as possible."

"The police are watching the airport," one of the detectives reported. "We gave them a picture."

Michael shook his head, chewing his lip. "They won't recognize him. He'll be disguised." He jumped to his feet. "You stay with Elizabeth," he said to the older detective. "Don't go out of the room, either of you." He looked at the other one. "We aren't leaving this to chance. We're going to the airport to watch every person who gets on a plane. He's barely had time to disguise himself and make it there. Let's go."

Tony Laperra fought the panic rising within him. He stood in a small store, sorting through the women's apparel.

"May I help you, sir?" A tall, heavyset American woman approached him.

His eyes swept over her. "I need a complete outfit for my wife," he said. "She's about your size."

The woman frowned and turned toward another rack of dresses. "You're in the wrong area. These are for us heavyweights." She led the way to the back of the store where several large dresses were displayed on a rack. She frowned, turning back to him. "You think she's my size?"

"Larger," he said. "Here, let me look."

Quickly, he flipped through the shapeless floral dresses, locating the longest one on the rack. "This looks right," he said. "And I need everything that goes underneath, plus dark stockings and a pair of shoes. Size eleven. And a handbag."

The woman hiked a brow. "She really is a big lady, huh?"

He nodded, glancing toward the front window where the crowd outside revealed only strange faces. "And I'll take this straw hat," he said, yanking one from a shelf.

"You'll want queen size hose, I imagine, and these are the largest shoes we have."

She handed him a pair of ugly black loafers. They looked too small for his feet, but he would manage. His life depended on it.

He nodded, taking the shoes and watching as she gathered up an assortment of items. She seemed to think of everything, choosing all the apparel in the largest size. He nodded approval. "Now just total it up. Oh, and she'll need a pair of those sunglasses." He pointed to the tortoiseshell glasses positioned near the cash register.

With his items in a sack, he left the store and headed for a service station across the street. The restroom was located outside the building, which suited him perfectly. Once he was inside the small men's room, he locked the door and began his transformation. Five minutes later, he deposited the clothing he had worn earlier in a wastebasket and awkwardly exited the restroom. A startled man waited to enter.

"Sorry, wrong room," Laperra said.

Dressed in women's clothes with sunglasses and hat, he hobbled down the street to the taxi stand, uncaring of the stares he attracted. He had glimpsed himself in the mirror and knew he looked comical. A tall woman in a long-sleeved floral dress on a hot day, with dark stockings and odd shoes. The shoes hurt his feet and made his limp more pronounced, but there was nothing he could do about that.

He had transferred everything from his wallet to the handbag, and now he was heading straight for the airport. Nothing in the hotel room would identify him, and he was too smart to return. His best means of escape was immediate. He flagged an approaching taxi, and it screeched to a stop in front of him. Clutching his purse tightly, he silently blessed himself for the woman's passport and birth certificate he carried in his wallet, folded into a tiny neat square. It would be the first time he was forced to use it.

Michael and the other detective, along with several local police, were covering the airport. Michael had ventured a guess that Laperra would choose the flight most remote from Atlanta to avoid suspicion. He was keeping an eye on the Los Angeles passengers since there were still seats available on that flight.

Suddenly a movement caught his eye, a slight limp in the gait of a boarding passenger. The passenger was a large, unattractive woman. At first he disregarded her. Then something about her made him look twice. Her big frame looked as though it were crammed into the ugly dress, which hung loosely about her waist and hips. She was the only woman in the airport with long sleeves and dark hose on this hot day, and she kept her head lowered, increasing his suspicion. All his senses went on alert.

Casually, he walked past the line of passengers, glancing at her. Her head swiveled in the opposite direction. He walked to the back of the line, then motioned for the police. The line moved forward and the big woman stepped to the ticket counter. As soon as he heard her speak, Michael knew this was a man masquerading as a woman. He'd bet his life it was Laperra.

The police reached his side and he indicated the suspect. Michael and the police stepped to her side, and Laperra whirled. The sunglasses dropped lower on his nose and Michael recognized the eyes.

"It's him," he yelled.

Laperra was not quick enough. They had him before he could run. One of the policemen grabbed Michael's arm as he lunged toward Laperra.

"Don't do anything you'll regret, Señor," the policeman said, shaking his head in warning. "We have him in custody. Let us handle it with the authorities."

"Don't let him get away," Michael ground through his teeth, glaring at Laperra.

The ugly woman's hat had been knocked from Laperra's head, along with the sunglasses. Now the entire airport was starting to react. Gasps and shouts filled the air; the passengers in line to the ticket counter scurried back from the fracas. Laperra was read his rights as he was handcuffed and led away by the Mexican police.

Michael followed them outside the airport. Laperra kept silent, saying nothing to the questions directed at him. After he was loaded into the police car, accompanied by the American detective, Michael ran to the taxi station. Foremost in his mind was getting back to Elizabeth. The immediate threat of Laperra was gone, but an even greater one waited somewhere for her. They had to find out where.

FIFTEEN

J ay sat in the interrogation room of the Atlanta Police Department facing Tony Laperra. The other detectives had aggressively questioned him while Jay planned his attack. He studied Tony through slanted eyes. He said nothing for several minutes, and Tony began to fidget. When Jay finally spoke, his voice was cool, calm, showing no trace of emotion.

"You're gonna love that prison cell, Tony. Attempted murder in Cancún, two more murders here in Atlanta, and—"

"You can't prove any of that."

"Oh, but you're wrong. You drive a black car, right?" Jay asked, already knowing the make and model. It was a real break in the case, for the black car could be used against Laperra.

Tony shifted uncomfortably in the metal chair. "I know what you're getting at, but I have an alibi."

"You consider a lady of the evening an alibi? Who do you think a jury will believe? Your flashy friend? Or a retired banker and his wife who were seated at the window of the restaurant when you drove by after your hit-and-run? Two people were killed, another was seriously injured, and you left them for dead. You're in big trouble, Tony."

For the first time, beads of sweat popped onto his high forehead. He was Italian and should have been handsome, with thick dark hair and dark eyes. However, the life he had lived was deeply etched in the lines of his face. His nose was slightly crooked, having been broken in a fight when he was younger. He certainly would garner no sympathy in court, no matter how smooth his defense.

He lunged for the one opportunity left. "Put me in a lineup. That couple can't identify me."

"Oh, I intend to put you in a lineup, Tony. And I'm quite sure they'll identify you. Of course, the woman wears thick glasses, so it's possible she could confuse you with someone else." Jay allowed a triumphant grin to slip over his face. "But I don't think that will happen. They've been pressured to come up with the driver, Tony. And you'll be the answer to their prayers, particularly since you drive a black car, and you dropped a switchblade only a few feet from Elizabeth Calloway in Cancún. Two detectives will swear to that. That's your second attempt on Elizabeth's life."

"I didn't do it!" he yelled, leaping out of the chair.

The door flew open and the detectives watching through the mirrored wall rushed in, ready to restrain him.

"You didn't do what?"

"You might have something on me in Cancún, but you can't pin that hit-and-run on me." His chest was heaving as he looked from Jay to the detectives.

"I think we can," Jay said coolly, looking him squarely in the eye. "But we have a lot of people here in the state who don't agree with capital punishment. What they'll prefer is life without parole. You aren't going to like it, Tony."

Tony sank back into the chair, glaring at Jay. "I don't have anything else to say until my lawyer gets here."

"You've already made your call and he's on the way." Jay stood up. "I think if he has any sense, he'll suggest you plea bargain. Who knows?" Jay threw up his hands. "You might tell us something that would tempt us to cut a deal."

Having dangled the carrot, Jay left the room without a backward glance. He had Tony Laperra right where he wanted him, and he loved it.

Once he was outside the room, the waiting detectives who had been watching and listening through the mirror frowned and shook their heads. "The Wallaces may not consider his black Honda a fancy new sports car."

Jay nodded. "Yeah, but he doesn't know that."

When Michael called his mother with the news that they were at the Atlanta airport, Ellie smiled, feeling both happy and relieved.

"Katie is doing fine. And Jay just called to say he has the guy right where he wants him. Whatever that means."

"That's good news," Michael replied, but he knew their work was just beginning. Laperra was only the middleman; someone else was involved, and Michael was anxious to get in on the interrogation.

"How's Elizabeth?" his mother asked anxiously.

"She's doing great, Mom. And thank God, the amnesia is clearing."

"Oh, Michael, that's wonderful news. I can't wait to see her."

"What I'd like you to do, Mom, if you don't mind, is drive Katie back to Oak Shadows and wait there for us. We'll be in sometime tonight."

Ellie ran her busy schedule through her mind, then quickly dismissed it in light of Michael's request. Crucial family matters took precedence over the church bake sale this afternoon.

"We'll be waiting, honey," she said tenderly. Her heart ached for what he had gone through. "And I'll have something special on the stove for you."

"Mom, I don't know what we'd do without you," he answered in a shaky voice.

"Darling, I'm more than happy to help you and your family. You know that."

After they hung up, she rushed out to the backyard seeking Katie. Mike had gone back to work at the garage today, and while she ran the vacuum cleaner over the house, Katie had dashed out the door to play with their dog, Sam.

She glanced around the backyard, expecting to see Sam and Katie at play. But Sam was alone, stretched comfortably under the big oak by the tire swing for his nap. Ellie lifted a hand to shade her eyes.

Katie was nowhere in sight. She called to her, but there was no answer. A sense of panic began to build in Ellie, though she told herself to remain calm. The trauma in the past weeks had taken its toll on the composure she once possessed.

Flying down the back steps, she began to check each corner of the yard, looking for Katie. She was nowhere in sight, even after Ellie called the second time.

She fought the panic rising within her, mentally scolding herself for even thinking of housecleaning when Katie was to be watched at all times. She tried not to think about what might have happened or what *could* happen, as her tennis shoes flew over the backyard, the front yard, then circled again to the backyard.

Far in the distance, way down by the lake, she thought she saw a movement under the big oak tree near the fishing dock. She began to run in that direction, her breath jerking in her chest. When she reached the tree and spotted Katie, her knees tucked up to her chest, her face buried in her arms, Ellie heaved a deep sigh and took a moment to catch her breath.

Katie had not heard her approach, because she was sobbing loudly. Ellie felt as though her heart would break when she considered Katie's feelings and recalled all she had endured in the past weeks.

Smoothing her hands over her jeans and clearing her throat

to announce her approach, Ellie took a seat beside Katie. She put an arm around her and gave her a hug.

"I bet you're missing your parents, aren't you, darling?"

Katie nodded, not lifting her face from her arms, though she had stopped crying.

"Then I have some great news for you! Mom and Dad are on their way home, and your mother is doing much better. They can't wait to get back to you."

Katie lifted her tear-streaked face to her grandmother. Her wet eyes were suddenly bright with hope. "Is Mom getting her strength back?"

"Yes, she is. I think she's going to be fine, Katie. And they want us to come home and wait for them."

Katie flung her small arms around her grandmother. "I've had a good time here, Grandma, but I'm ready to go home."

"I know you are, darling. You've been such a brave little girl, and we're all so proud of you. But I know how it feels when you get homesick. Sometimes I get homesick for this old farm, believe it or not. And I know you miss Brooke."

Katie said nothing; she merely hugged her grandmother tighter.

"So if you want to get your things together, we'll make our plans and head back home."

Katie pulled back and looked up at her grandmother. Her blue eyes held the sheen of tears, but now there was gratitude on her face. "Thank you, Grandma."

"You're welcome, Katie." Ellie smiled down at her with a heart overflowing with love. Katie was smart and perceptive, like her parents. For the first time, it dawned on Ellie just how much emotion Katie had been holding inside while she tried so hard to be a big girl, a brave girl who pleased everyone around her. And she had.

"Now, shall we go back up to the house? Maybe while I cook some food to leave on the stove for Grandpa, you could play with Sam one last time. He's going to miss you."

"I'll miss Sam, too," she said, wiping her face and looking around the yard. "Maybe you can bring Sam over to spend a week with me sometime."

"Good idea," Ellie said with a tap on Katie's shoulder.

As Katie skipped ahead, Ellie thanked God that at last there was some relief to their torment. All of them had been carrying a heavy burden, especially Michael. She prayed that life would get easier now. Of course, Jay had called with the good news that an arrest had been made, but he had told her nothing more, and this puzzled her. Still, she knew it was the rule of a good detective not to divulge privileged information, and her sons were the best.

The story had made front-page news by the time Michael and Elizabeth returned to Oak Shadows. The unsolved hit-and-run was a hot topic, and the fact that such a notorious criminal was still on the loose had spun a web of tension over Atlanta and the surrounding counties. Even the police in adjoining states were watching for a black sports car with a dented fender. When a leak came from the police department that an arrest had been made, everyone waited with bated breath.

Especially the man holed up in his den, pacing the floor, watching the driveway for his supplier. He had called his administrative assistant for the third morning in a row, updating his illness from mild to serious. The doctor had threatened to hospitalize him if his condition did not improve. No, she should not bring chicken soup or send anyone over. The greatest favor she could do for him was to cancel his appointments and allow him the privacy to recover. He needed bed rest and was not to be disturbed.

He had to make a decision, and he had to make it with a clear head, he knew that much. No more cocaine, not for a while, even though every ounce of his body begged for relief. He had a sense of being out in a desert, stumbling around in a desperate search for water. This was even worse. And all the while, he knew there would never be a high like the first one. But for some reason, he kept trying, hoping, yet finding only a temporary escape from his mounting problems. He ran his hands through his thinning hair and tried to think. It was only a matter of time until they broke Laperra, and when they did, he would tell them everything.

The man sank into his chair, his head buried in his hands. What was the smart thing to do? He ran through numerous options, discarding all of them for one reason or another. At one time, he had been the best in his profession, but now everything he had spent thirty years working for could go down the drain. He would rather die than have that happen to him.

One slightly comforting thought kept circling his mind as he pondered his circumstances. He had a very important client coming to town for a private consultation. That appointment and subsequent ones could mean big bucks. They would add to the hefty balance in his savings account. He could afford the very best defense. But what would it take to ease the ache within?

All the money, the power, the status—all had failed to fill the empty spot in his soul, a hole that seemed to grow deeper with each passing year.

Out of nowhere, the words of his long deceased mother rose to his mind, a eulogy to chastise and torment him.

"Only God can fill the void within your soul."

She had spoken those words to him as he worked three jobs to put himself through school to earn his various degrees.

He lifted his throbbing head from his hands, vaguely taking note of the clamminess of his palms. Where was his supplier? He didn't like the direction his thoughts were taking. It was too late for a stab of conscience.

Anxiously, he got up and paced to the window, staring across the huge manicured lawns toward the entrance. He was still in his silk pajamas and leather house shoes, because he was too distraught over needing the drug to get dressed. This served the purpose, however, of convincing his household staff that he had a virus.

Soon, he hoped, he would see the van coming up the drive. It was neat and deceptive, a security service coming to check out the house. He had purposely set the burglar alarm off twice now, just to prove the system should be checked on a regular basis. Either there was something wrong with the wiring or someone was trying to break in. This was enough to make everyone eager to see the van appear; they would even greet the guy warmly as he entered with his tool chest.

It was all a farce, of course. The tool chest was exactly that, ironically. The "tools" he carried kept the man's sanity intact, and he sensed he was slipping closer to the edge each day.

But for now he had to think, he told himself, although his nerves were jagged and his hands were trembling.

Jay Calloway. He was to blame for this. He had personally escorted Laperra back from Cancún after two detectives had caught the idiot attempting to close in on Elizabeth Calloway. And he had no doubt the Calloway brothers would live up to their reputation as the best detectives in Atlanta. He had seen them prove that beyond a doubt. It was just a matter of time until Calloway broke Laperra.

Then another thought came to him—something he hadn't considered before. He couldn't threaten Laperra, it was way past that. But he could alter the investigation. If Jay Calloway's mind was diverted, if there was a serious threat…yes, that was it. It was his only chance to save himself. Once Laperra heard what was going on, he would know that he was being taken care of. Maybe he would keep still until someone could get to him. And someone would.

The man who drove the van had the type of low-life contacts who could take Laperra out once he was released on bail. But first there was Jay Calloway to deal with; he had to be diverted from his interrogation until Laperra was out on bail.

The van turned slowly into the driveway, and the man's body began to tremble more violently. He couldn't wait for the white powder to fill his senses, calm him down, obliterate his pain. But he wasn't foolish enough to think the pain would end with the cocaine. No, he had to make this decision while his head was clear.

He walked to the door and yelled for Emily, the upstairs maid.

"Tell the security guy I'm in my bedroom. I'm considering the necessity of installing a device up here."

"Yes, sir." The girl scurried toward the stairwell, eager to deliver the message.

When the supplier entered the bedroom, toolbox in hand, the man had a wad of bills waiting for him. The guy opened his toolbox, grinning. This man was keeping him in business, the kind of business he liked. If this continued, he would soon be buying a condo and a boat at the marina, down in Panama

City. His eyes bulged at the wad of bills, much more than usual.

"Yeah, ten thousand," the man said. "But it's not all *security money*," he barked, using the code for the white powder. "I have another little job for you."

"One that's worth the extra five grand?"

"And then another ten grand when it's completed."

The guy was fascinated. He set down the toolbox, momentarily forgetting his mission in light of a more lucrative enticement. He licked his dry lips, his mind leaping with curiosity. "What do you have in mind?"

The man despised the sly grin that slipped over the hoodlum's face. He was the kind of trash the man hated, but he had no choice. He was in over his head and he knew it. And if necessary, this idiot would be tossed to the sharks at a later date.

"It's a simple job if you do exactly as I tell you. But if you bungle it…" His gray eyes cut across the man's face like a steel blade.

The guy sat up straighter in the chair. "For fifteen grand, I'll do what you want, and I'll do it exactly the way you tell me."

The man took a deep breath and sat down in his favorite wing chair.

"Oh, do you need—" He reached down to open the toolbox.

"No, I have to explain this clearly, so I'll wait a minute on your delivery. And next time, bring twice as much."

The guy straightened, focusing on the man before him. The habit owned him now, he could see that from the sweat pouring down his face, the shaking hands, and the unkempt appearance. But he listened carefully, ever mindful of the money he had been offered.

"The job I have for you is going to be easy, if you do it

right," the man said, taking a deep, shaky breath. "So listen carefully."

SIXTEEN

Tracy left the market thinking of the special dinner she and Jay would share this evening. She had bought steaks for Jay to grill, potatoes she would bake, and ingredients for a healthy salad. Afterward, they would drink decaf with just a dollop of whipped cream. She hugged the bulging sack tighter against her stomach, and the baby kicked in protest.

"Okay," she laughed, thinking he or she did not want to feel left out. "I have some low-fat yogurt so you can get your calcium." Glancing around, she laughed to herself, thinking how ridiculous she must look, talking to herself as she walked across the parking lot. It was midmorning, and the parking lot wasn't crowded—only a scattering of moms like herself, shopping for the day's needs.

She reached her car, dived into her deep shoulder bag for the car keys, and unlocked the door to the new white Ford Jay had bought for her birthday. There was plenty of room for the baby's carriage seat, and the trunk was quite spacious.

She turned the key in the lock of the door, placing the sack of groceries in the passenger side of the car. It was easier to get them this way, rather than leaning into the trunk. Her large stomach forced her to make all kinds of new concessions.

Slamming the door, she crossed to the driver side and opened the door, wedging herself in beneath the wheel. Only five more weeks to go, maybe less. The doctor was guessing on an early delivery, and she and Jay were having fun studying the calendar, trying to figure out which day their little bundle of joy would arrive.

Because her thoughts were centered on happy things, it took her a second or two to realize the car wasn't starting. She frowned, pressing harder on the accelerator. Only an odd ticking sound answered. Was it the battery? She was about to reach for the phone when she spotted a familiar truck turning into the parking lot. It was the service truck for the garage they used, and he was driving into the next row, parking. A man in overalls got out, started toward the grocery, then cast a glance in her direction.

She hesitated for only a moment, realizing his face was not familiar. Probably a new guy Mr. Fisher had hired.

He was looking directly at her, as though he recognized the car, and she began to wave to him.

In quick strides he hurried to her car, looking polite and helpful. "You're one of Mr. Fisher's customers, aren't you?" he called to her.

"Yes, I'm Tracy Calloway, Jay's wife."

"Yes ma'am, I know Jay. What's the problem?"

"I can't get my car started."

"Let's have a look. Want to pull the hood latch?"

"Sure."

Again she thought about calling Jay, but what was the point? She liked taking care of her problems herself, even though Jay wanted her to rely on him. But she kept reminding him she had lived in L.A. for two years, was a successful reporter there and—

The man had taken a look at the engine and was now walking back to the driver side window. "Want to try it again, Mrs. Calloway?"

"Sure." She turned the key in the ignition, mentally crossing her fingers, but the same sickening click answered back.

He shook his head, removing a handkerchief from his back

pocket to wipe his hands. "I'm afraid you may have a serious problem, one that we'll need to discuss with your husband."

Tracy frowned. "What's wrong?"

"It's the engine. Looks like we'll have to replace a part." He glanced at the groceries. "Got anything melting in that sack?"

She glanced at the groceries. "Yes, I do."

"Then let me drive you home. I'll come back and tow your car to the garage. I'm sure Mr. Fisher will discuss the problem with your husband as soon as we determine what's wrong."

She hesitated. Her back was beginning to hurt, and it was a hot, muggy day. She longed for the air conditioning of their little house.

"In fact," he said, looking pointedly at her stomach, "I think you'd better get in out of the heat. If you don't mind my saying so, you're not looking too well. Your face is flushed, like your blood pressure might be up." He gave her a broad grin. "My wife and I have three kids, and I know all about the situation. My wife complained a lot," he said with a chuckle, "but I didn't mind. We had three healthy babies."

Tracy smiled. He was a nice guy, so likable and friendly, and she was grateful to have run into him at such a crucial time. "I want a healthy baby, more than anything. And we don't really care if it's a boy or girl, just so long as everything goes okay."

"Then let me drive you home. You don't need to be worrying about your car or anything else. Let's just get you back to your comfortable sofa where you can put your feet up. You can call Mr. Calloway when you get home and let him know what's going on. After I drive you home, I'll come back and tow your car to the garage."

She tilted her head and smiled at him. "That's very nice of you. I really appreciate it." She was glad she'd had the good fortune to run into a man with children; it made him more understanding of her condition.

As he opened her door, she shifted her weight and got out of the car. He reached into the car for her groceries. "We don't want to forget these. As hot as it is today, something could melt or spoil in no time."

She nodded. "You're right."

She followed him to the tow truck and allowed him to help her into the passenger seat. Then, groceries in hand, he came around to his side and got in, carefully placing the groceries between them. She smiled at him.

"I really appreciate this."

Predictably, the lawyer had advised Laperra to say nothing more. Someone was posting the enormous bond required to get him out of jail.

"Come on, Calloway," he snarled. "You gotta back up your accusations before you can hold him without bail. And you haven't done that yet."

"I'll have done it in a couple of hours."

"We'll see," the lawyer said.

Jay nodded. If Laperra did get out on bail, Jay knew the best men on the force would be watching him around the clock. His phone was bugged, and a detective had temporarily taken residence next door to Laperra's condo. Everything Laperra did and said would be monitored.

Violating his rights, some would call it. In Jay's opinion this guy had no rights. He was linked to a man who had killed two people, almost killed his sister-in-law, and then put a contract on her head.

The disgust Jay felt for such a lowlife overrode the rules of his job. He didn't care if he was suspended or fired for overstepping boundaries. He was going to see that Laperra and his boss got the justice they deserved.

Wearily he drove home, trying again to reach Tracy on the car phone. When the answering machine came on again, he frowned. He had tried to call her around three, when she should have been back from her shopping. There was no answer, and the closest he came to talking with her was listening to her voice on the machine and then leaving a message at the beep.

"Hey, Tracy. I'm worried. Where are you, hon?"

His frown deepened and he drove faster.

Then he remembered that Michael and Elizabeth were flying in today. Maybe she had taken some groceries up to their place and lost time in a conversation with them. It would be unlike her to do that without first checking in with him, though, not because he expected her to account for her every move, but because they had been warned that the baby might be early. She did not drive far without first telling someone where she was going.

He dialed the number to Michael's house, but at first there was no answer. Then, to his surprise, his mother answered.

"Hey, Mom, are they back yet?"

"No, but they'll be here soon. They called from a service station about half an hour ago. Katie and I are cooking supper now."

He nodded, thinking. "Have you heard from Tracy?"

"No…why?" His mother's tone changed, instantly picking up the concern in his voice.

"Oh, no reason. Knowing her, I thought she might have taken off up there to check on them."

"Oh, I see," she laughed. "Yes, that's typical of Tracy, but no, she hasn't called. Should I ask about the investigation?"

"I'm on my car phone. Let me call you back when I get home."

"Good. We'll be waiting to hear."

Jay was nearing his home as he hung up. Still, he was feeling a bit anxious. Had she gone to the doctor? Then another thought occurred to him, and he smiled to himself. She'd been hanging out at a specialty baby shop only a few blocks away. He had probably just missed her between the grocery store and shopping there.

Relieved by the thought, he glanced idly at the homes he passed—small, cozy ranchers like the one he and Tracy had recently bought. It was a safe neighborhood with the majority of residents being young couples buying their first homes.

He turned into the driveway of their quaint little brick home, and automatically glanced toward the garage. He did not expect to see her car since she was not answering the phone.

He pulled over to the side, giving her ample room to park when she returned. Tonight he was grilling steaks, and Tracy was planning a candlelight dinner.

Reaching for his briefcase, he got out of the car, glancing around the small yard. The grass needed to be cut on Saturday. Perhaps by then they would have this case tied up. Then he would be able to catch up on work at home that had been neglected.

Unlocking the door, he stepped inside the neat foyer and entered the den, dropping his briefcase in the chair beside the desk. He headed for the kitchen, eager for some of Tracy's mint tea. The house was still and quiet, and he was so accustomed to having her here, waiting for him, that he found his spirits sinking when she was not home to greet him.

His eyes were drawn to a large note on the kitchen table.

But even from a distance, he could see it was not Tracy's handwriting. He walked over and looked at the note, written on a page ripped from a blank TO DO list on the wall.

The scrawl on the note hit him squarely between the eyes, and for a moment, he had to grip the back of a chair for support.

The words were brief and concise, delivering the most frightening message he had ever read:

If you want to see your wife and baby alive again,
you will call your dogs off Laperra and do nothing
more to torment him until the case comes to trial.
DO NOT call the police or try to find her.

The black ink swam before him; for a moment he thought he would faint. He found himself thinking of Michael that night at the hospital. He would never forget the expression on Michael's face: one of helplessness and despair. Jay felt all of that and more now, for Michael could at least walk down a hall and touch his wife; she had been in the hands of skilled physicians.

But Tracy…and the baby…they were in the hands of monsters, and he had never in his life felt so helpless.

Michael! Michael would help him. He glanced at his watch. Were they home by now? He was afraid to trust anyone at the Department. Someone must have leaked some information; the abductors knew too much. Somewhere there was a mole in the organization. Laperra and the man behind him were as notorious as any criminals he had ever dealt with, because life had no value to them.

He sank into a recliner, his head in his hands, and he began to pray. *God, tell me how to handle this. And please, please take care of my wife and baby until we can find them.*

Jay called fifteen minutes after Michael arrived home. Michael could tell from the tone in Jay's voice that something was terribly wrong.

"Michael, I need you to come down here immediately. Don't worry. Elizabeth is safe, but that's all I can tell you for now. Michael, don't say anything to anyone at your house. This has to be kept confidential."

Michael nodded. "Okay, pal. I'm on my way."

He made an excuse to his family. There was an emergency at his office that only he could handle.

He tried to avoid his mother's questioning eyes, and it was hard to say good-bye to Elizabeth, for he was unsure exactly what was going on. But the two detectives were here at the house, and they had earned his respect in Cancún by saving Elizabeth's life.

"I shouldn't be gone long," he said, trying to sound light-hearted as he kissed Katie and Elizabeth and rushed toward the door. He stopped before stepping out. "Mom, we haven't seen enough of you lately. Why don't you spend the night to give us a chance to catch up?"

Ellie looked pleased. "Well, if you want me to, I suppose I can call Mike." She glanced at her watch. "It is getting a bit late for me to drive back to Moonglow."

"Great!"

With that Michael was out the door and into his car, hoping he had managed to carry off his departing speech without arousing suspicion. Once he was in his car, he dialed Jay on his phone.

"What's going on?" he asked.

"I'm getting ready to check out a little problem with the kitchen sink. But you can still borrow my putter for your golf game."

"Okay, thanks." Michael hung up his car phone and frowned. Either Jay was afraid the phone was bugged or someone was already in the house. Had Jay called earlier from a pay phone? Should he call for backup in going into Jay's house? He was torn with indecision as he sped toward Jay's neighborhood. The one warning Jay had given lingered in his mind and he decided to heed it.

This has to be kept confidential.

He drove past Jay's house, seeing only Jay's car parked in the driveway. Tracy's car was gone; that sparked a warning in his mind. His gut told him this had to do with Tracy. If anyone was inside, he would simply have to run the risk of that danger. Jay needed him; that was the most important consideration. Jay had never failed to come when Michael called him, and now he could do no less.

He backed up and pulled into the driveway, studying the exterior. Twilight was descending over the quiet neighborhood. All seemed so peaceful and serene, but from Jay's words, Michael knew that was not the situation at his brother's home.

He got out of the car and strolled up to the house, acting as though nothing were wrong. He even stopped momentarily to admire Tracy's hanging ferns. If anyone other than the neighbors watched him, he hoped his casual demeanor would divert any concern. Slowly he opened the door and called out to Jay. To an onlooker he seemed as normal as ever, but inside he was a bundle of nerves.

"Come in, Michael," Jay answered.

Jay strode down the hall to meet him, his face pale, his features drawn.

Michael stepped in and closed the door behind him, staring into his brother's face.

"What's going on?" he mouthed the words.

179

Jay motioned him toward the kitchen. "Want something cold to drink?" he called.

"Er, not now, thanks."

Once they were inside the kitchen, Jay handed the note to Michael. Michael read the note, his eyes widening in horror as he glanced momentarily from the note to Jay, then back again.

Wincing, he laid the note back on the table and laid an arm around Jay's shoulders. "Do you think the place is bugged?" he mouthed again.

"Probably," Jay whispered back.

Michael nodded. "Jay, I didn't just stop by to borrow your putter," he said loudly. "I also wanted to invite you and Tracy over for dinner this evening. Can you make it?"

Jay managed to make his tone of voice resemble that of one pretending not to be distraught. "Tracy…uh, Tracy's out shopping now, so I can't speak for her. We'll have to, er, think about it," he added with emphasis.

He walked across to the cabinet drawer and withdrew a legal pad. "Michael, I'm pretty busy, so if you don't mind, I have to get back to fixing the kitchen sink." He shoved the pad toward Michael.

Michael read the words already written there. *What do you think I should do? Laperra is due to post a million-dollar bond and get out late today.*

Michael picked up the pen and wrote: *Then we'll have to stop him from getting out. He's our link to Tracy.*

"Well," Michael said, sounding regretful, "I'll tell Mom you're not sure about dinner." On the pad he wrote: *They know we're getting to Laperra, that he'll confess everything if he's kept longer. By grabbing Tracy they think you'll back off the questioning. Insist on talking with her; we want to know she is safe.*

"Man, I appreciate the use of your putter. If Elizabeth is

feeling okay, I may go out to the golf course tomorrow. After the stress I've been under, I need to play some golf. It always relaxes me."

"Sure." Jay managed to sound indifferent. He walked to the hall closet and made a lot of noise shuffling through the golf bag. "Here it is." He handed him the putter and mouthed, "Thirty minutes."

It was an old code they used for meeting on the eleventh hole at a remote course south of town. They could talk freely there and perhaps devise a strategy. "Well, good luck with your game," Jay finished.

"Come for dinner if you can."

"We'll see after I talk with Tracy."

Michael walked out of the house, putter in hand, and closed the door behind him. It was hard to look casual knowing the state of mind his brother was in at the moment. He stopped to pet the dog; then, whistling nonchalantly, he strolled down the sidewalk to the car, examining the golf putter along the way.

Inside the service van parked down the street, a man sat behind the wheel, observing Michael. Another man was seated in the back of the van, replaying the conversation between Jay and Michael.

"The guy doesn't look worried," the driver called to his companion, who was rewinding the tape again, listening to the bugged conversation.

"Doesn't sound worried either. But don't you think it's odd that the other Calloway just dropped by?"

"Yeah, but if it was a real meeting, they would have chosen another place. I think the guy is doing exactly as he was told."

~ ~ ~ ~ ~

Michael thought his emotions had run the gamut over the past weeks, but now he found himself thrust into another crisis. Fear mixed with anger when he thought of Tracy, helpless and pregnant, in the hands of these ruthless people, whoever they were. One thing was for certain now: more than one person was involved. And it took big money to synchronize all the deception, the intricate plans.

He drove along, eyes narrowed in concentration. Who in the city of Atlanta could have been at Nick's restaurant, committed the horrible crimes, then followed up with Laperra, one of the most deadly hit men in the country? But Laperra had one weak spot, and they knew what it was: jail cell claustrophobia. He would not go back to prison. If he got out on bail, he would be killed; if he stayed in jail, he would talk. Eventually. But so far his highly paid lawyer had been able to wrangle bail on the grounds that he had not been positively identified as the man who committed the crimes at Nick's restaurant.

Elizabeth!

She was the key. He had tried to shield her from this, fearing it would do her harm to sit through a lineup. She recalled the accident now, right up to the car, but the driver was still a blank.

He thrust his hands through his hair as he pulled to a stoplight. When was this nightmare going to end?

When they found the man behind the nightmare! And that had to be soon—very, very soon.

SEVENTEEN

Elizabeth and Katie walked across the backyard, hand in hand, their faces wreathed in smiles.

"Mom, I'm so glad you remember me," Katie said, looking up at her mother with adoration in her bright blue eyes.

"Oh, honey," Elizabeth sighed, "I'm so sorry for not remembering you." She stopped walking and knelt beside her daughter. "The injury to my head wiped the important things out, but only for a while. I could never forget you for long," she said, tweaking Katie's cheek.

"Well, I'm just glad you're well now."

"Yes, everything is going to be fine," Elizabeth said, coming to her feet again. *It will be fine when I remember the face of the man,* she thought, wishing desperately she could put that final piece of the puzzle together. Michael and the doctor kept telling her the man's face would come to her memory in time, just as everything else had done.

"You were telling me about the garden there." Katie pointed. "About how you and your grandmother used to plant flowers, and then when we moved back, you and I planted flowers. Remember?"

Elizabeth squeezed her hand. "Of course. The garden was one of the first things I remembered when we came back to Oak Shadows."

She hesitated as her eyes wandered over the landscape.

"Katie, I'm fortunate to have had a home. Not everyone has a place to return to, a home and land that holds good childhood memories. For me, this was the real gift, and it's one I want to pass on to you. Oak Shadows is more than just a beautiful estate, although we're very proud of what we've done here. The important thing is that this land was bought and the house was built by our ancestors. There's lots of history here, and lots of love. Your father now feels that comfort when he comes home."

She hesitated, looking down into her daughter's wide eyes. "Oak Shadows is a place I've returned to many times in my mind when I was away from here, because it gave me a safe, secure feeling. I want you to have that."

Katie nodded and turned to look around her at the neat long square of lawn, the borders of petunias circling the trees, the swing her dad had hung from a low oak limb. In the distance, her parents were having a small fishing lake built for everyone to enjoy.

"Mom," she sighed, "I'm so glad the bad things are over."

Elizabeth nodded and smiled. She would remember the man's face, she knew she would. It was only a matter of time.

Jay had managed to lose the man who had been tailing him for the past thirty minutes. He had parked his car at the market, gone inside, asked the manager, who was his friend, to borrow his car. Then he had gone out the back door, jumped into Marty's car, and taken off to the golf course to meet Michael.

Michael was stationed at the eleventh hole as planned, half-heartedly attempting a shot. His eyes constantly searched the grounds for anyone suspect. When he spotted Jay walking toward him, Michael withdrew the small binoculars from his shirt pocket. The binoculars were sleek and high-powered, displaying everyone on the golf course and even in the parking lot.

"Nobody arrived before you came or since," Michael said as Jay approached.

"Good," Jay replied. "I lost the guy tailing me."

"Okay," Michael began, speaking quickly. "I've thought it through. Here's what we have to do. We have to inform Judge Walton that Tracy has been kidnapped so that he will deny Laperra bail. Remember—" he put up a hand as Jay began to protest— "Andrew is a friend of the family. We can trust him. He hasn't been well lately, but he's back at work now. He'll be the one who decides if Laperra gets out."

Michael heaved a sigh. "Another thing. I've decided that Laperra should be put in a lineup so Elizabeth can identify him. She can be sure he's the man who was in the car, maybe temporarily. We're going to have to trust her with this as well, Jay."

"Michael, Elizabeth is just now getting better. I don't want to put her at risk again." ·

"She's at risk as long as he's out there, Jay. Never forget that. And now with Tracy—" he broke off.

Jay pressed a hand to his temples, trying to soothe the throbbing headache. He couldn't bear to think of the danger to his wife and his unborn child.

"So if Judge Walton knows about Tracy, and then the detectives and Elizabeth link him to Cancún, he'll deny bail. I think Laperra will start to panic and be more willing to cut a deal."

Jay nodded slowly. "You're right. Can you talk to the judge?"

Michael nodded. "Right away, and we'll arrange a lineup. You may have been warned to back off, but not me. I'm going after him now before they can do anything else, Jay. We'll have Laperra identified and put the squeeze on him right afterwards. Add this sequence of events to the fact that Elizabeth's memory is clearing...." He reached out and clamped Jay's shoulder. "We'll have the man's name soon. That's a promise." He extended his hand and they shook.

Jay fought back tears of gratitude as he gripped his brother's hand and felt the strength flowing back into his own body. "What do guys do without brothers?" he asked shakily.

"After all you've done for Elizabeth and me, I honestly don't know. But keep your chin up, pal. The worst will soon be over. I'm back on duty and I won't rest until we nail him. Now get back home and wait for the phone call."

He nodded. "I've called in sick to headquarters. So if anyone's checking, they know I've eased up on Laperra."

"And I'll put Elizabeth in a safe house if necessary," Michael added.

"And Katie," Jay said, looking worried.

Michael couldn't bear to think of that, but he knew he must. They were dealing with a dangerous, sick man, perhaps several. It might even be some type of conspiracy, but his instinct still maintained the person behind all of this was a rich, powerful man in Atlanta who could afford to pull strings.

"Jay, I'm on this harder than before. So just go home and let me take over for a while," Michael said.

Jay nodded, turned, and hurried off toward the back of the clubhouse.

Michael leaned down and picked up his golf ball, dropped it into his bag, then scanned the scattered group of golfers. Nobody else had come around. He had to pray their conversation had gone unheard. Now it was time to talk with the judge and then arrange a lineup. He walked briskly toward the clubhouse, seeking a telephone.

By five-thirty that afternoon, Elizabeth sat in a small, enclosed area staring through the mirrored wall to the stage where several men would enter in a matter of seconds. Michael sat beside her for he, too, was a witness, along with the other two detectives. The assistant DA and the chief investigator had set things up and were now present. When the door opened and instructions were given, six men walked across the platform.

Elizabeth's eyes flew to the man in the center: the tall, dark-haired man with large features and a slightly crooked nose. She looked quickly at Michael, who pressed her arm gently, indicating that she should wait until the procedure was finished.

She tried to take note of the other men who stepped forward, faced front, turned right and left, in the customary pattern. Still, she was unable to keep her eyes from straying back to the man she had seen at the market, the man with the knife. Was he the one in the car? No, he wasn't. But he was the link to man. The main job for her now was to identify Tony Laperra.

She fidgeted in her seat as the other men stepped back in line. As soon as the tall, dark-haired man stepped forward, she turned to the assistant DA and nodded vehemently.

He nodded in reply, and Laperra stepped back in place. Two other men came forward and repeated the procedure.

At last it was over and they all tromped out. The lights were turned on in the room where Elizabeth and Michael were seated. The chief took a deep breath and turned to face them. "So for the record, what is your conclusion?"

Michael nodded. "The man in the center of the lineup is the man who dropped the knife meant for Elizabeth. I chased him for three blocks before losing him."

The chief nodded and looked at Elizabeth. "And you?"

"Yes, the man in the center is the one who tried to kill me in Cancún. I'm absolutely certain."

Michael knew the two detectives who had gone to Cancún had already identified Laperra; now Michael had repeated the process with Elizabeth.

"Can she leave now?" Michael asked, looking worried.

He nodded. "I think so. Tom," he said turning to the investigator, "you're to do the necessary follow-up and I'll report this immediately to Judge Walton. The judge reminded me the guy has run out on bail before. He shouldn't be released on bail."

Michael was already whisking Elizabeth out of the room. Everyone in the Department knew how Laperra had evaded them in the past. There was no question now that bail would be denied, and so it was time for Michael to move in.

"Sir, in Jay's absence, he's asked me to interrogate Laperra."

The assistant DA shook his head. "Can't let you do that, Michael. You know the rules. You were directly involved. But you needn't worry, the most aggressive team in the Department will be talking to him. I understand the judge is about to go out of town and wants this thing settled."

"Believe me, so do we," Michael said as they turned for the door. He hurried Elizabeth down the corridor and out the back door, where a limo with tinted windows waited. Two of the best detectives on the force were accompanying Elizabeth and Katie to Florida. Jack Newman sat behind the wheel while Tom Robinson was engaged in a lively conversation with Katie.

Michael leaned into the car. "Katie, you've been wanting to go to the beach. Now's a good time for you and your mother to spend a couple of days at a condo down there. You still agreeable?"

Katie was ecstatic. She had been overjoyed at the news that she and her mother were going to a condo at Seascape. Her only regret was that she could not take Brooke, but Mom had promised that for another time.

Michael helped Elizabeth to the car and gave her a kiss. "I'll see you soon. In the meantime, you'll be well taken care of." He nodded at the two detectives. It was all part of the disguise to get Elizabeth and Katie out of Atlanta and to a safe house before word leaked to the man that Elizabeth had identified Laperra.

"Bye, Dad," Katie squealed, and Michael leaned farther into the car, kissing her on the cheek.

"Bye, honey. Have fun, and stay close to Mom."

"I will. I promise."

"Michael, be careful." Elizabeth gripped his arm, and he could see that she was fighting tears. "I don't know if this will help, but when I think of that awful night..." She swallowed hard, then continued. "I see that black car in my mind, and I find myself thinking of Julie Waterford."

Michael hesitated. "Why do you suppose you do that?"

She shook her head. "I don't know. But I do. Always."

Michael turned that over in his mind. "That's interesting. Keep thinking about it and I'll look into it, as well."

Julie Waterford had been their neighbor at Oak Shadows and had suffered from dissociative identity disorder. She had led them on quite a chase in search of a missing twin who had died years before.

"We need to go," Tom prompted as the windows were rolled up.

Michael stepped back from the limo and looked around the parking area. It was now six o'clock, and Laperra was still under interrogation.

As the limo pulled out of the parking lot, Michael felt a momentary pang of discomfort, even regret. The detectives taking his wife and daughter were the most careful and professional of all the detectives, in his opinion. He was certain they could be trusted to take excellent care of Katie and Elizabeth. And yet, until the man behind this case was arrested, Michael was not prepared to trust anyone completely. Not with his wife and daughter, who were his entire life.

He turned and walked briskly back into the police station. He had promised Jay he would not leave unless he got a coded phone call from him. So far none had come. His thoughts flew to Tracy, and he silently prayed for her safety. It had been the utmost prayer in everyone's minds. So much had happened since noon, when she had been abducted. There had been no word from her, and by now Jay was getting frantic. But word would soon come; they had to keep their hopes up.

In the meantime, Michael had some thinking to do. Why had the memory of Julie Waterford come to Elizabeth's mind when she thought of the car? There had to be a connection. What was it?

Tracy had no idea where she was, but she could smell something being fried—meat, French fries, something. She was blindfolded and seated in a recliner, which was reasonably comfortable. She wore a ski mask over her face and tape around her wrists, but she had been fed and treated with more consideration than she had expected.

The ski mask was dark but still she could make out a faint light through its ribbed surface. She had tried so hard to see something, but she could not. So instead she tried to focus her attention on the voices of the man and woman, but they were hushed and distant.

She had spent the first hour crying tears of fear, then frustration, when she realized she had been tricked. She knew this latest incident would only add to the problems Michael and Elizabeth were having.

The baby. She had to think of the baby. It took every ounce of her energy to remain calm when she wanted to scream or fight back, but she had to think of the baby. The more upset she became, the more difficult it could be for both of them.

When she had settled into the service truck earlier, thinking she was on her way home, the man had locked the doors and then pulled out a gun and told her to keep still. Terrified, she was unable to speak for several seconds. Then, realizing she was being abducted, she began to sob, hating herself for showing emotion, yet unable to refrain.

"Lady, you'll be better off to stay calm, not upset yourself, and not upset me," he warned.

She looked across at him, wondering belatedly why she had ever gotten in the truck with him. He was a thin, lanky guy with mousy brown hair and pale brown eyes. What was she thinking of, riding off with him? Angrily, she vowed not to give him the satisfaction of asking how he obtained the truck or any other details that might compliment his scheme. Her instincts as a reporter came back to her now, and she tried to revert to the calm and objective nature that had made her successful in her job. She had been unable to read the man, and she chose to remain silent, hoping he would speak up, and by doing so, reveal more about himself. Then she might have a better idea of how to react to him.

She tried to follow the route, but he had turned into an alley, tossed a ski cap at her, and told her to put it on.

"Don't you think I might attract a little attention riding around with a ski mask over my face on a summer day?" she retorted.

"Just do as you're told," he snapped back, pointing the gun at her stomach. The gesture was effective, and she obeyed.

He then made another turn and she could hear a door opening and closing. The truck tires seemed to be moving smoothly over the surface. A concrete surface? The traffic was muted now. If she had to guess, she would say they were inside some sort of warehouse or garage.

The truck slowed. The engine was turned off. The seat squeaked as his weight shifted, and she straightened, her senses trained for every sound. His door slammed, creating an odd echo. Yes, they were inside a large area. His footsteps were approaching the passenger side, and her back stiffened as the door beside her was yanked open. She felt a gust of hot air sweep into the truck.

"Okay, take it easy stepping down," he said. She felt the pressure of his hand around her arm as she thrust her feet out and slid down from the truck. The heat and the trauma of what was taking place swept over her, and for a moment she thought she was going to lose her lunch. She thrust her head back trying to get a deep breath through the knit of the ski mask.

"Come on," he said impatiently as her footsteps lagged.

"I can't see where I'm going," she argued back.

"That's the idea," he snorted.

A metal sound creaked beneath them, and she stumbled as they entered someplace. The door slammed behind them and she jumped, unable to calm her nerves.

"Okay, just walk over this way."

"Slow down with her." It was the voice of a woman, and Tracy thought she heard a note of sympathy in her tone. She thanked God there was a woman present, and that this one seemed to have some compassion when the man did not. She heard a key turn in a lock somewhere.

Another hand gripped Tracy's arm, a smaller, gentler hand, the hand of the woman. "There's a recliner right over here," she said with a slight twang. "Just take small steps…you're almost there."

Tracy's knee bumped something soft and she stopped.

"Good. Now turn around and sit down," the woman instructed.

Guided by the stranger's hand, Tracy reached back behind her with her foot, feeling for the sides of the chair. The fabric was soft yet ribbed, and she pictured a faded corduroy recliner. The cushion made a light swoosh as Tracy finally sank into it.

"Now lift your feet and I'll get this footrest fixed for ya," the woman said. Tracy heard the rusty groan of a lever and felt the footrest swing up to support her feet.

Tracy moaned softly, feeling the relief of finally getting her swollen ankles elevated.

"Do ya want somethin' to eat?" the woman asked. "I can make you a sandwich."

"No." Tracy shook her head. "But I'm thirsty."

"I'll get you a beer. No, I don't reckon you want a beer. Want a can of pop?"

"Can I have some water?" Tracy asked, wondering if she was taking a chance on being drugged. If not drugged, she wondered how dirty the cups would be.

"Never mind," she said.

"No, I'll get ya a cup of water."

The woman left, and Tracy leaned her aching back against the chair, feeling the baby give a swift kick.

It's okay, little one, she thought, swallowing hard. *We're going to be okay. We have to believe that.*

"Here's yer water," the woman said, rolling the ski mask up above her mouth so she could drink.

The woman's fingers moved gently and Tracy realized this woman had far more concern for her than the man had.

Tracy's wrists were bound with tape, making it awkward to hold the cup. The woman helped as Tracy's fingers groped around the sides of the cool cup, something that felt like

Styrofoam. The woman helped her guide the cup to her lips, and the water cooled her parched mouth and slid down her dry throat.

"Thanks," she said, releasing the cup after she had drained it.

The woman's footsteps made a splatting sound on the floor. Like bare feet on concrete, Tracy thought, wondering who on earth these people were.

She could hear the man talking in a low voice across the room. She cocked her head to the side, trying to hear what he was saying, but he was talking too quietly to be understood from a distance.

Heavy steps thundered across the floor, the lock clicked again, the door opened and slammed. She heard the truck start up.

"Is anyone here?" she called out.

"I'm here but I'm watchin' my program, so just rest now."

Her program? Then Tracy heard the vague sound of something familiar, a popular commercial. The woman was watching television on the far side of the room.

Tracy twisted her hands against the tape. It held tight. If only she could reach up and yank the ski mask off! But she knew that would be foolish. She did not want to make the woman angry. So far she had been treated okay, especially since the woman took charge of her.

She settled back in the chair and tried to think clearly. She could talk to the woman, maybe outsmart her, once she gathered her wits.

"My husband is a detective," she called out. "The best. He'll find me. Then you'll be an accomplice to kidnapping. You do know that, don't you?"

The woman snapped something back at her; then there was only the droning sound of the television. But she *had* snapped,

Tracy told herself smugly; the remark had pricked her nerves. Tracy had made her point and at least given the woman something to think about. *Or perhaps she was only irritated that her television program had been interrupted,* Tracy thought with a sigh.

She pressed her head against the seat and tried to pray. Then she remembered the poem in her pocket, a special poem written by a friend. She had planned to give the poem to Elizabeth, but perhaps it could be used now.

"Will you do something for me?" Tracy called.

"What do ya want?" The woman's tone was skeptical.

"I have a poem in my shirt pocket. Will you get it out and read it to me? Please? It will help calm my nerves."

There was a moment's hesitation, then footsteps crossed the room and a hand darted inside Tracy's pocket.

"A Prayer to God." The woman spoke hesitantly at first, then her voice picked up as she read the poem aloud.

Where do I go from here? Is it far or is it near?
Help me, Lord, so I can hear.
I have walked this road alone so much,
Please help me, Father, to stay in touch.
You are all I have along the way;
Shine your light on me today.
If you want to know what I'm trying to say,
Oh Lord…I have lost the way.
Maybe, Lord, you want me to give in to you today
So you can carry me the rest of the way.

The woman's voice trembled on the last line, but she said nothing more. Tracy felt the poem being tucked back inside her shirt pocket. The woman's footsteps retreated.

Tracy heard the roar of an engine, then the slam of a door. She tensed, waiting. There was a soft rap on the door. Again feet splatted and a lock clicked.

It was the same man, talking in a low tone to the woman.

"...and time to call Calloway."

Tracy's breath caught in her throat. Were they going to call Jay?

She bit her lip. She must not start blubbering once she heard Jay's voice. She had to be brave, let him know that she was all right so far. But how long would that last? And what could she possibly tell him to let him know where she was? She had judged them to be no more than a mile from the market, then inside some garage or on a basement level of a building. How could she convey that to him without setting the man off in a fit of anger? Her mind chewed on the possibilities. When finally a phone was shoved in her hand and she was told to speak, she swallowed hard.

"Jay?"

"Tracy! Are you all right?" His voice was shaking.

"Yes, I'm okay. They're treating me well. But I didn't get the steak you wanted at the market. I was fifteen minutes late and—"

The telephone was jerked from her hand. "You've talked to her. Now follow your instructions," the man barked and hung up.

Tracy sat very still, wondering if *market* and *fifteen minutes* had conveyed a message that she was about fifteen minutes from the market. Jay had a sharp mind; maybe he had picked up the tip. This was her only hope. If the kidnapper had caught on, she ran the risk of his anger.

"He sounds scared," the man said to the woman. "I think we'll have this little job over with in no time."

Their footsteps retreated, and Tracy concentrated on the sounds. They must be eating now, for she could hear a rustling sound—paper plates shuffling, maybe—and the smell of food was stronger.

The woman was saying something about being scared. The accomplice bit had frightened her, just as Tracy had hoped it would.

"All we're to do is hold her, Shelly, so calm down," the man snapped, his voice rising in anger.

Tracy took a deep breath. So, their job had been to abduct her and hold her until further notice! But she had seen the man's face; she couldn't believe they would allow her to go free after that.

"...be out of town by tomorrow." His voice was slightly muffled, as though he spoke with food in his mouth.

She had heard correctly! He had been hired to abduct her, let her make her call, then at some point he and his woman would leave for parts unknown. *He must have been paid well,* Tracy thought bitterly, again wondering who had the kind of money it took to pull off all that had happened. There were many millionaires in Atlanta; if she were still a reporter, she would be tracking the man from that angle. Why didn't they think of that? Or perhaps they had.

She sighed, feeling weary. The baby kicked, and again she reminded herself that she had to try to relax. From what she had heard, they were not going to kill her. She and the little one were safe, just a bit uncomfortable. What could she do to make her situation better?

Then, recalling her upbringing as a pastor's daughter, a memory came to her. Once she had talked to her mother about being frightened.

"Darling, just pray the prayer I prayed when I was in the delivery room trying to bring you into the world."

"What's that?" Tracy asked curiously.

"Take a deep breath and say, 'Dear God,' release the breath and say, 'please help me.' Not only does it tend to relax you, it instills peace of mind."

She began to do that, silently praying, *Dear God* as she inhaled, and *please help me* as she exhaled. After a few deep breaths, she began to feel the tension seeping from her body. God would help her; he had helped her before, and he would help her again.

Tony Laperra was covered in a cold sweat. He had been ID'd and now bail was denied. It was only a matter of time until he was dragged into a courtroom and tried for double murder, hit-and-run, and two attempts on Elizabeth Calloway's life. It didn't matter if this fancy defense lawyer could get him life without parole; he'd rather have the death sentence.

Maybe Jay had backed off, but now the others seemed to be closing in, and there was no word from his boss. He had expected him to do something more than squelch Jay, but he was not going to do that. In fact, he was going to let him take the rap!

With the man's power and money, he could hire other witnesses to place Laperra at the scene of the crime; he could escape conviction by making Laperra the fall guy, and he was ruthless enough to do that!

Laperra's imagination was working overtime now, and cold sweat poured from his face. He wasn't going to take any more of this, not for some lousy rich guy who could buy and sell half of Atlanta!

"I want to talk to my lawyer!" he yelled. "I may have some information for Calloway!"

EIGHTEEN

Tracy realized she must have dozed off when she heard the telephone ringing in the background.

The man was muttering something; then his voice rose in an angry shout. "You'll get no more goods from me until the money is in my hand. And what do you expect me to do with the woman?"

Tracy's breath jerked through her chest as her heart began to hammer. Something was going down, as Jay would say. What did the man mean about getting no more goods until the money was in his hand? And what about her? What was going to happen to her?

Quick steps flew over the floor to her side, and the woman was gently touching her hand. "I'll make a deal with you, okay? You never saw my face so you don't know me. You don't know my voice, either. Right?"

Tracy nodded. "Right—if what?"

"If I call your husband and tell him where to find you."

"Please." Tracy could no longer hold back the tears. "I promise I won't ever try to identify you. I don't know you."

A hand squeezed her arm. "I have a baby boy," she whispered, "and I didn't agree with you being treated this way, but—"

"Come on." The man's loud voice shot across the room. "We gotta go now. Leave her right there."

Footsteps flew out of the building; something clattered in the wake of their departure, like a chair being kicked over. The smell of fried food still lingered in her nostrils, and she fought back a rush of nausea. She couldn't let herself come apart; she couldn't be sick. But telling herself that did nothing to abate the feeling.

She tugged against the tape on her wrists and felt it loosen. Had the woman loosened it? She tried sawing it back and forth, back and forth, and she felt it loosen even more. She continued to work at it until her hands were free. She could hardly believe it. Her fingers flew to her face, yanking off the ski mask.

For a moment her vision was blurred; then slowly the room came into focus. It was a long rectangular room with the recliner in which she was seated and a TV tray beside it. At the opposite end of the room were two straight chairs, a portable TV on an upturned crate, and a hot plate and skillet with the remains of something fried. Paper plates were squashed into a garbage can. Otherwise the room was empty.

She pressed her hands onto the arms of the faded brown corduroy recliner and pushed herself upright. She stood on shaky legs and looked around, seeking the phone they had used. Then she decided it must have been a cellular phone, because there was nothing else in sight. She was alone in the room—and she was free!

She ran toward the door, expecting it to be locked, but to her surprise, it opened when she turned the knob. It was dark outside, but she could see that she was in a dimly lit underground parking deck. There were no cars parked here.

Suddenly she heard a siren wailing in the distance and she leaned against the door, waiting. It was Jay coming for her, she knew it! The woman had kept her promise.

Jay's car screeched to a halt, and the door flew open. He raced across the parking lot to her, tears in his eyes. Neither spoke as she dissolved in tears against his chest. For a moment there were no sounds except her sobs and his words of comfort. Then the baby gave a hard kick, letting them both know that they were not the only ones glad to be free.

NINETEEN

The minute Michael got the call from Jay, he bolted out of the police station and jumped into his car. He had been going over everything in his mind for a clue as to why Elizabeth would be thinking of Julie Waterford. He had tried to reach Julie at the hospital where she was recovering, but she had gone to bed early and was not taking calls. Who was left to consider? Her husband was deceased. Something nagged at his subconscious. Like Elizabeth, he felt something simmering just under the surface of his thoughts, but he couldn't define what it was that bothered him.

The clinic. He thought it had something to do with the clinic.

He began to drive toward the private clinic where he had sneaked inside while working on the Julie Waterford case. One thing about that case kept bothering him: had Dr. Waterford, Julie's deceased husband, loved her, or had he used her as a guinea pig for his research on her disorder?

Soon he reached the upscale neighborhood where homes and elite businesses were grouped together, looking cozy yet prosperous behind tiny halos of streetlights. Turning down Marshall Drive, he drove slowly past a clothing store and a portrait shop. The porch light was on at the clinic highlighting the front steps. In the back, a streetlight offset the shadows. He turned into the driveway and drove around to the rear parking lot, and then as he stared at the empty parking spaces, it hit him.

He and Elizabeth had met with Dr. Waterford's partner from the clinic. His name was Dr. Phillips. They had come upon him in the parking lot of the country club following a charity benefit. Phillips had been alone and was hurrying toward his car as they were leaving. He seemed not to recognize Elizabeth until she introduced herself and reminded him that she had met him when she came to speak with him about Julie.

"Oh yes," he had said, stopping to look at her curiously. Then his attention turned to Michael as she introduced them.

Dr. Phillips was a small man, fiftyish, with long, uneven features and gray eyes that probed from behind frameless glasses. Michael had experienced the same reaction to him that Elizabeth claimed to have felt. He did not particularly like him.

"I understand you've helped Julie," he said in a clipped tone. "I'm glad to hear that." He glanced again at Michael. "Nice meeting you." Then he whirled on his heel and hurried off.

Elizabeth had glared after him. "He didn't acknowledge her case or give me a chance to say anything about it, did he? You'd think since she had been the wife of his colleague at the clinic, he would have said something. But he was a cold fish the first time I met him, too."

"Come on, hon," Michael said, reaching for her hand. "We're running late."

Elizabeth was still staring after the doctor when they reached their own car. Then she had said something rather odd. "Quite the sport, isn't he?"

He had interpreted her remark as sarcasm, but now he remembered hearing a car leave the driveway. A sports car. Could he have been driving a black Jaguar?

Michael's mind was racing as he drove around the building and came out on the opposite side. It would be easy to find out if he had owned a Jaguar. He glanced back over his shoulder as he pulled into the street again.

He checked his watch. Elizabeth would not be in Florida yet. They were to call when they were safely in the condo. That should be a few hours from now, and he did not want to upset her in the middle of the night. He'd wait until first thing the next morning to confirm his suspicions.

In the meantime, he was going to find out everything he could about Dr. Phillips.

The man sat very still in his bedroom, trying to decide what to do. His source at headquarters had already warned him that Tony Laperra was ready to talk and that Tracy Calloway had been released. They were now after the man who had abducted her. And nobody seemed to know where Elizabeth Calloway was.

Mrs. Calloway is the only reliable witness against me, he thought. *She is the only one who can place me at the restaurant. If there were other witnesses, I would have heard about them.*

He could hire witnesses against Laperra and the drug dealer. Who would take the word of a thug over his, with his solid reputation to stand on? He pushed himself out of the chair, glancing at the clock. It was after one. He had to get a good night's sleep so he could think straight. Tomorrow he must be smarter than he had ever been; his life depended on it.

The sprawling condominium complex was located in a quiet area of Panama City Beach, away from the tourist crowd. It was after eleven when a guard at the gate looked with interest at the limo. Tom and Jack had switched driving and now Tom was at the wheel. He rolled down the window and presented their pass.

Katie had thought it was fun riding in the limo, but now she was stretched out on the backseat, asleep with her head in Elizabeth's lap. They pulled into an underground parking deck and parked near the elevator.

Elizabeth noticed how cautious the men were once they had parked. Both got out, inspected the parking deck and elevator, then unloaded their luggage from the trunk of the car.

"Wake up, sleepyhead." Elizabeth kissed Katie on the forehead.

Katie stirred. "Hmmm?"

Elizabeth glanced at her watch. It was ten minutes after eleven. "We're finally here, but it's late so we need to go up to the condo and get in bed."

Tom opened the door beside Elizabeth. "You two ready to go up?"

Katie was half asleep, hanging on to Elizabeth's arm as they got in the elevator and rode up six floors to their condo. When the elevator opened, the men checked the quiet, carpeted corridor leading past several doors. Jack unlocked the end door, turned on the lights and looked around while Tom stayed close to Elizabeth and Katie.

Elizabeth was pleased with the condo. A mirrored foyer led into a large living-dining area, with a small U-shaped kitchen tucked in the rear. It was furnished with modern pieces, deep cushioned sofas and chairs done in yellow and white, and matching draperies across the end wall. Tom walked over and drew the curtains, unlatching the sliding glass doors that overlooked a balcony and the ocean.

"All the comforts of home." He smiled back at them as the cool ocean breeze drifted in through the open door. He closed the door, latched it again, then indicated a large room on the right. "That's the master bedroom and bath with lots of closet space. You and Katie will want that one. Jack and I will take the two smaller bedrooms and bath on the opposite side."

Elizabeth nodded, leading her sleepy daughter into the master bedroom. Like the living area, this room held modern furnishings, a huge, comfortable-looking bed overlaid with a lush blue spread to match the draperies.

The phone in the living room began to ring as Elizabeth was opening Katie's suitcase to find her nightshirt. Katie had already sunk onto the bed. "Come on. Let's get our teeth brushed," she urged. Katie reluctantly pulled herself up and went into the bathroom.

There was a knock on the door. "Michael's on the phone," Jack called.

"Thanks." Elizabeth hurried to the phone on the bedside table and lifted the receiver. "Hi, Michael. We made it just fine."

"Great. And I have some wonderful news. Tracy is back with Jay, safe and sound."

Elizabeth released her breath in a deep sigh of relief. "Oh, thank God. When—"

"About eight this evening. I wanted to wait until you were safely in the condo to call. She's been able to give a good description of the man who grabbed her, and there's an APB out for him now."

"Is she okay?" Elizabeth spoke with a soft voice, hoping Katie hadn't heard from the bathroom where the water was running.

"Jay says she's just fine. Now listen, honey, I want you to get a good night's rest. I'll call again in the morning. We may have a break in the case, but I don't know yet. Just get some sleep and we'll talk first thing."

"All right. Michael?"

"Yes?"

"I love you."

There was a momentary pause and then she heard the tenderness in his voice. "I love you, too. Very, very much."

She nodded. "You get some rest."

"I'll try. Now put Jack or Tom back on, please."

She went to the door and opened it. The men were in the kitchen, unloading a sack of groceries. "He wants to speak to one of you."

Tom nodded and grabbed the kitchen phone.

She closed the door just as Katie returned to the bedroom, her blonde hair slightly tousled, her eyes fixed on the bed. Elizabeth went over and turned back the covers and Katie hopped in and nestled down, closing her eyes.

Elizabeth smiled tenderly at her, thinking how simple life was for Katie in many ways. She longed to protect her from the harsh realities of the world, but she knew someday Katie would have to face them as well. As parents, Elizabeth and Michael could try to instill their Christian values and teach her how to find divine guidance. Beyond that, there was a limit to what they could do when she grew up and went out on her own.

Elizabeth closed her eyes for a moment, unable to think of that now. She could hear the soft swish of the surf spilling onto the shore. She walked over to lift the draperies and peer through the glass doors to the balcony.

The condominium complex had plenty of night lights, and she had seen the security guards patrolling when they drove toward the parking deck. She felt safe here. She stared out at the dark, vast ocean and breathed deeply of the warm, moist air. She wondered what tomorrow would bring.

The next morning Elizabeth awoke early as the morning sun slipped through a crack in the drapes. She glanced across at her daughter, curled into a little ball beneath the sheets. Katie lay on her side, facing Elizabeth, her head snuggled into the pillow. A lock of hair draped over her right cheek, and as Elizabeth looked at the pert little nose and soft mouth, pride swelled in her heart. She thanked God for the blessing of her husband and daughter, and for the fact that her life had been spared.

Michael. Her thoughts moved back to Atlanta, wondering what was going on. She was so grateful that Tracy had not been harmed. The threat of danger slipped over her, making her restless, and she gently turned the covers back and slipped to the chair, hugging her knees to her chest. Every morning, first thing, she searched her mind, hoping the night had magically restored the last missing fragments of memory

For the hundredth time, she replayed the scene at Nick's restaurant; it always seemed like a nightmare. She remembered turning into the restaurant…driving around back to park…another car pulling out…then the speeding black car. But still she could not see the man's face.

The familiar panic shot through her when she realized she could turn the entire case around by simply remembering that face. She bit her lip in frustration. When was this going to clear? She got up and went to her suitcase, searching for the day's outfit. She chose a pair of white shorts with a blue-and-white striped T-shirt. Gathering up what she needed for a shower, she slipped into the bathroom and closed the door.

When she returned, dressed for the day, Katie was sitting up in bed, looking around.

"Hi, Mom!" Her blue eyes were bright after a night's sleep, and her small face looked eager with anticipation.

"Hi, darling. Come look." Elizabeth walked over and drew the drapes. "Now that it's morning, we can see the view we have, and it's wonderful."

From their sixth-story height, it was as though they had

stepped out into the morning with the seagulls, surrounded by blue skies and sun-sparkled blue water. The sky was a clear blue with only a few baby clouds rolling around out on the horizon. Directly below them, the waves tumbled gently toward the shore, making white scallops against the sand.

"I want to go out," Katie said, yanking at the glass door.

Elizabeth started to stop her, wondering if it was safe. Then, looking out, she realized they were perfectly safe. No one could get to them at this height.

"Okay." She unlatched the glass door and slid it back.

The warm morning breeze wafted into the room, billowing the curtains. Elizabeth stepped outside with Katie and felt the tangy salt of the ocean breeze touching her face. It was going to be a hot day, with plenty of sunshine. Already a few couples were out strolling the beach. A woman and a little boy were building a sand castle.

"Can we go looking for seashells, Mom?" Katie looked up at her hopefully.

Elizabeth hesitated, wondering exactly how confined they must be. There had been little chance to discuss their options on the way down. It had been a long, tiring trip and everyone was too exhausted to do more than say good night.

"We'll see. Hungry?"

"Just thirsty."

"Then wash your face and comb your hair. After you're dressed, we'll have some juice and maybe take a walk."

Katie was already diving into her little suitcase, tumbling through the contents.

"Hold it, young lady," Elizabeth said, laughing. "All your carefully packed clothes will be nothing but wrinkles, the way you're going."

Katie had already pulled out the shorts and matching top

she wanted to wear, along with a pair of flip-flops. "Can we go swimming later?"

"Maybe."

Katie tossed out her bathing suit and beach towel. She didn't seem to mind that this trip differed from their usual romp at the beach. Elizabeth had to remember to be careful, and yet she wanted Katie to have a good time. This was their first chance to be together doing something fun since her accident.

The sound of the television in the other room reminded her that the detectives were with them. Everything was going to be okay.

When Katie was dressed, they entered the living room where Tom and Jack sat on the sofa, watching the news on television.

"Good morning." Elizabeth smiled.

"Morning." They nodded pleasantly. They were already dressed for the day in shorts, T-shirts, and flip-flops. Although their clothing was fresh, their faces held the weariness of long hours on the job. Jack had only been given an hour's notice that he was to accompany them to Florida.

She smelled coffee and turned toward the kitchen. It was a small, compact room, done in black and white. Her eyes moved from the coffeemaker and microwave to the stove and refrigerator. Tom had made a dash into a grocery when they arrived to pick up milk, juice, coffee, and fruit.

"You guys want some juice?" Elizabeth called as she located glasses in the first cabinet.

"No, thanks." Tom held up his coffee mug, indicating he had what he wanted.

"Maybe later." Jack smiled.

Elizabeth poured orange juice for Katie and herself as Katie plopped down on a stool at the counter.

"Going to be a nice day," Tom called as he watched the weatherman detail the day's forecast.

"Katie, are you a surfer?" Jack teased.

Katie giggled. "No." She reached for her orange juice, glancing back at the men. She seemed to enjoy having them along. Elizabeth was thankful that Katie seemed unaware of the grave circumstances surrounding their trip to the beach.

She sipped the fresh orange juice, enjoying its tang, while her thoughts moved back to Atlanta and Michael. He and Jay were working so hard, along with the police force and numerous detectives. At least Tony Laperra was in custody, and they were after Tracy's kidnapper. Maybe today would bring some good news. She had identified Laperra, but then she had Michael and other witnesses to confirm her identification. There seemed to be nobody but her to identify the mystery man.

She finished her juice and poured herself a cup of coffee. Michael had said she mustn't beat herself up over it; everything would fall into place in time. She wondered if he really believed that.

"Can we go looking for seashells now?" Katie asked, setting her empty juice glass down on the counter.

Elizabeth sipped her coffee and glanced toward Jack. "We'd really like to go for a walk on the beach. We'll be fine," she added, hoping to reassure them.

"I'd like to take a walk too, wouldn't you, Tom?"

Tom still looked half asleep but he appeared to be trying to muster up some enthusiasm. "Er, sure."

Elizabeth wished that she and Katie could go alone, but she knew it wasn't sensible. The men had to follow the orders they had been given and play watchdogs.

"I'll get my treasure bucket," Katie said, hopping down from the stool and rushing toward the bedroom.

Elizabeth washed the glasses and coffee cup, dried them with a paper towel, and put them away. She looked across at the men. "I guess you guys need a break, too."

She realized this was work to them, and she mustn't forget to acknowledge her appreciation. They had wives and children back in Atlanta, and she knew they were wishing they could be here with their families rather than having to work.

Katie rushed back in with her small orange bucket and a little sun hat perched on her head. Soon they were all trailing down to the beach for a walk in the bright sunshine.

Feeling the sun on her face and stepping into the sand, Elizabeth recalled her trip to Cancún with Michael. It had been such a wonderful time, a time of healing and getting to know one another again…until Laperra showed up.

"Mom, look at this one," Katie called enthusiastically, as she knelt to retrieve a cone-shaped shell.

"That's pretty." Elizabeth nodded. "Want to keep it?"

Katie hesitated. "I'll keep it until we find some prettier ones." She deposited it in her bucket and skipped merrily ahead. "Mom, I'm hungry!" she called over her shoulder.

Elizabeth was about to tell her to eat one of the granola bars they had brought when she spotted a place just down the beach. It was a pale pink, Victorian-style house enclosed by a white picket fence that advertised SEASCAPE, BED AND BREAKFAST.

She smiled. "That looks like fun. You guys want to have breakfast there?" she called back to them.

"Sounds good to me."

Katie was already skipping up the walk, obviously enchanted by the house that had been converted to a bed and breakfast.

A young woman had walked out onto the porch and was smiling as they approached.

"Hi, I'm Jessica Castleman. I own this place. Won't you come in?"

"Thanks. I'm Elizabeth Calloway and this is Katie."

Tom, the older detective, cleared his throat loudly, a warning to Elizabeth she was not to reveal her identity. She wasn't worried, however; the kind expression in the woman's dark eyes made her feel she could trust Jessica Castleman.

"Today's specialty is blueberry muffins and ham omelets," Jessica said, looking toward the men. "Does that sound good?"

"Great," Tom said, quickening his steps.

They all tromped up onto the porch and entered the charming house. Elizabeth looked around. On both sides of the hall were parlors that had been converted to breakfast rooms. A few people sat together, talking quietly, looking as though they were enjoying themselves. She felt safe here, but still she was not hungry.

"I want to eat in this room," Katie said, rushing into the room on the right. It was filled with seashells and driftwood and lovely paintings of seascapes.

Everyone followed, then stopped when Katie chose a table with only three chairs. Tom and Jack turned toward another table.

"Why don't you two join Katie? I'm really not hungry," Elizabeth said.

Jessica had tilted her head and was thoughtfully studying Elizabeth. "I was just having a cup of herbal tea over there." She indicated a small table in a far corner. "Would you care to join me, Elizabeth?"

She nodded. "Yes, thank you."

Jessica turned back to the men. "Have a seat, and a waitress will be right with you."

Katie had already settled into one of the ladder-back chairs and was looking through the window to the beach.

The men settled into the chairs beside Katie, but Tom continued to watch Elizabeth.

She merely smiled, appreciating his protective nature. She turned back to Jessica. "Thanks for inviting me to join you," Elizabeth said under her breath. "The idea of breakfast was for their benefit, not mine."

Jessica nodded, as though she understood, as she led the way back to her table. "How about tea and a muffin?"

Elizabeth nodded. "I suppose so."

Jessica gave her order to a waitress as Elizabeth took a seat and looked around. On one wall, she spotted a photograph of Jessica and a man, obviously her husband. Jessica wore a white dress and veil and the man was dressed in a tux. He was tall with sun-streaked brown hair and friendly green eyes. The couple stood on the porch of this house, and Jessica was holding a colorful bouquet of roses.

"That's my husband, Mark Castleman," Jessica stated proudly. "We were married out there on the porch, with only family and close friends present."

Elizabeth nodded. "You look very happy."

"We are. And that's a lovely diamond ring you're wearing," Jessica said, admiring Elizabeth's ring.

Elizabeth glanced down at the ring she had put back on her finger as soon as she returned to Oak Shadows from Cancún.

"I have a wonderful husband too," she said, then was unable to restrain a sigh. "We've been through a lot the past year."

"Oh?" Jessica glanced toward the men seated with Katie.

"He isn't over there. Those guys are just...friends."

Jessica seemed to take this in stride. "You said you had been through a lot. So had I when I met Mark. I was a widow, trying to restore this house—" her small hand swept the interior of the lovely home—"and having a rough time of it. God literally dropped Mark in my path, right out there on the beach."

"Really?" Elizabeth looked at her curiously. She needed to avert her mind from her problems, so she tried to focus on this pleasant woman, who appeared to be about her own age.

"Yes," Jessica continued freely. "We had some problems to work through as well, but it was worth the effort. I've never been happier!"

She was a lovely woman with olive skin, dark hair and brown eyes. Elizabeth thought this woman was the essence of grace in the way she spoke or gestured or moved across the room. She was wearing a sundress with a brown background and dark imprints of seashells across the dress. It was ankle length, and tiny black sandals covered her feet.

"Here's your food," Jessica said as a small waitress placed Elizabeth's tea and muffin before her. The waitress gave her a brief smile before hurrying off.

The muffin was freshly baked. Elizabeth picked it up, thinking she might be hungry after all. "This is delicious," she said.

"The salt air does wonders for one's appetite." Jessica smiled at her.

Elizabeth nodded. She was suddenly feeling better.

"Where are you from, Elizabeth?"

"We're from Atlanta."

"I have friends from Atlanta. I'm from Angel Valley originally—"

"Angel Valley!" Elizabeth exclaimed. "Up in the Smokies?"

"Yes." Jessica laughed. "So far as I know there isn't another place by that name."

"It's my favorite tourist spot." Elizabeth smiled.

"You and lots of other people," Jessica replied. "Even though the people there try to discourage tourist traffic."

Katie had sailed through her breakfast and was crossing the room to their table.

"My pancakes were great," she said, smiling at Jessica.

"Thanks. I'm glad you enjoyed your breakfast."

Elizabeth reached up with her napkin to dab at the syrup on Katie's chin. "You can see that she did," she said, laughing.

"How big is your house?" Katie asked as her eyes rolled around the room.

Jessica smiled. "Would you like to take a tour? I'll be glad to show you around."

Before she could respond, Elizabeth saw Tom heading toward their table and knew it was time to go. "We'll take a raincheck," she said. "We have to get back to the condo. My husband will be calling."

Elizabeth touched the linen napkin to her mouth as she stood. She felt she needed to make some sort of explanation to Jessica. "My husband is a detective who finds missing people. He's working on a case." She bit her lip, hearing Tom's sigh. She hoped she hadn't revealed too much information but she felt an explanation was needed. They made an odd-looking group.

"Excuse me," Jessica said, "but you say your husband finds missing people?"

"Yes, he has an agency, Searchers."

"Then you two might want to take a trip up to Angel Valley. A woman up there has been reported as missing, and the little town is most upset. Your husband might be able to help, and you could see your favorite spot again."

Elizabeth lifted an eyebrow. "That's a thought. Maybe I'll mention it to Michael."

"If you want more information, call me. Or he can call the police up in Angel Valley."

"Could we head back?" Tom prompted.

Elizabeth nodded. "Of course." She turned back to Jessica. "It's been a pleasure meeting you."

"The pleasure was all mine." Jessica followed them to the door. "And please do come back."

"We will," Katie called over her shoulder, heading out to the porch to retrieve her bucket of seashells.

"Let your mom get them," Jack said, turning to Katie. "I'm challenging you to a race."

Katie giggled and took off running. Elizabeth picked up the bucket, suspecting this was planned to give Elizabeth and Tom privacy to talk.

Tom turned to Elizabeth. "I didn't mean to rush you, but Michael said he'd be calling around eight-thirty. I just wanted to be sure we're back at the condo, even though I have a cellular phone with me."

She nodded. "You're right. I'm really anxious to talk with him. He told me last night he may have a break in the case this morning. I hope that's what he tells us when he calls."

Tom nodded, staring down the beach. "So do I, Elizabeth."

With a manila envelope tucked under his arm, Michael hurried through the door of his new office in Marietta. He smiled at Anita Jackson, his secretary, already at her desk though it wasn't yet eight-thirty.

"Good morning, Anita."

She was a tall woman in her fifties with salt-and-pepper hair, a few wrinkles bracketing her eyes and mouth, and a pair of soft brown eyes.

"Good morning, Michael. The coffee is hot."

"Great." He hurried over to pour a cup from the coffeemaker into his mug. He had slept only a few hours, then rushed to the newspaper office first thing. He remembered a recent write-up on Dr. Phillips regarding a book he had done, and the picture in the paper had been clear. He now had the picture in the manila envelope along with a confirmation from Jay that Phillips had owned a black Jaguar.

"How are you?" Anita asked, looking him over.

"Busy." He turned his attention to the new office equipment he had installed for Anita and himself when they moved to Marietta. He had invested in an electronic scanner that had proved invaluable in scanning photos that he often faxed to another location. He handed the manila envelope to Anita.

"We need to scan this and then fax the copy to the condo in Florida. While you do that, I'll make a phone call."

Anita nodded, taking everything in stride.

Michael hurried into his office and circled his cluttered desk to the chair. Placing the coffee mug on the desk, he grabbed the telephone and dialed the number of the condo in Florida.

Tom answered on the first ring.

"Hi, it's Michael. Everyone okay? Good. Listen, I'm going to fax a photo to Elizabeth. I'll send it to the business office there at the complex and you or Jack pick it up, okay? This may be the man Elizabeth saw that night, so stay close to her in case she gets upset. Thanks. Yeah, I'll talk to her now."

"Hi, honey," he said, leaning back in the chair and releasing a deep sigh. He was always grateful to hear her voice, to know that she was okay. "Now listen, I have something to discuss with you, and I want you to think about this clearly. Can you do that? Okay. Do you remember the man who was in partnership with Dr. Waterford at the clinic? Dr. Phillips?"

Elizabeth frowned, clutching the telephone. "Yes, I just met him that one time when I went to talk with him about Julie Waterford." She suddenly felt anxious and nervous. What did Michael have to tell her?

"You and I saw him again recently at that benefit for the children's hospital," he reminded her. "You remember we met him in the parking lot at the country club?"

Elizabeth gripped the phone tighter. She was seated on the bed in the master bedroom with the door closed, talking on the extension. Directly in front of her, she had a tranquil view of the ocean, and she knew she needed that view now, for suddenly her head was spinning. Did she remember what he was asking her?

"Think carefully, Elizabeth. We went to the benefit for the children's hospital. It was on a Friday evening and you wore a new spring outfit. Blue, I think. We came out of the club and just as we crossed the parking lot, we met Dr. Phillips. He was leaving. You introduced him to me, but I had the same reaction as you—I didn't particularly care for him."

She nodded slowly. It fell in place with the blue suit. She remembered buying it specifically for that occasion. It was a warm spring night, the flowers were blooming, there was a nice fragrance in the air. She and Michael had gone to the club and he had complained about the crowd. There were cars everywhere.

"Dr. Phillips. Oh yes." She spoke slowly as the man began to come into focus. "He wasn't very friendly, was he? And he seemed to be in a hurry that night."

"Elizabeth, that night in the parking lot, you said something about him being a sport as he was leaving. Do you recall what he was driving?"

Elizabeth caught her breath, her thoughts tumbling backward. The parking lot, the BMWs, the Mercedes, a few modest cars. He was driving away in…

"A black Jaguar!" she cried, leaping off the bed. "Michael, that's it," she cried, tears filling her eyes. "He may be the one who was driving the black sports car at Nick's restaurant."

"All right, now listen to me. At this moment, Anita is faxing a copy of a photo of Phillips down to the condo office. Look at the picture carefully, then call me back. In the meantime, is this doing anything to jog your memory?"

She nodded, her heart racing. "The night of the hit-and-run, I saw the driver from the side, then his head turned…. Michael, I believe I'll know when I see the picture but…yes, it's very possible it was him. I remember he was not an attractive man when I met him. He had cold eyes. On this night, the man driving the car had a glazed look in his eyes, like maybe he was drunk."

"Or drugged," Michael said. "They've just picked up a man at the Georgia-Alabama border who matches the description of the man who kidnapped Tracy. He's a known drug dealer."

"Oh, Michael! Is it possible this nightmare is about to end?"

"I think it is, sweetheart."

Just then a knock sounded on her door and Tom poked his head in. "Jack just brought this up from the office."

"Wait, Michael. Here's the picture."

Her fingers were trembling as she reached for the copy. She held the paper, still warm from the machine, and stared down into the face. She gasped. "Michael, it's him. I know it's him!"

"Don't panic." Michael's voice came back, calm and steady. "Jay is taking another copy of this photograph to the woman who was seated at the window. She may not be much help, but Phillips has a distinctive nose. She may remember him. In the meantime, will Katie be too upset if you come right back home? In fact, I'm going to ask Tom to put you two on a plane and I'll meet you."

Elizabeth began to nod. "Yes, let's not waste another minute."

"Fine. Let me speak to Tom. And Elizabeth…I love you."

"I love you too, darling."

She handed the phone to Tom and sat staring at the photograph. The man had a thin face with narrow, beady eyes behind frameless glasses, a long nose, and a tight little mouth. As Tom spoke in the background, she slipped over to a chair by the sliding glass doors, holding the photograph to the light.

She thought back to the day she had gone to the clinic to see Phillips. She had been distressed about Julie Waterford, and he must have known that. Yet he sat aloof behind his desk with all of his framed diplomas surrounding him. Despite his status, he had seemed to be lacking something essential. And now she knew what it was. He had no heart.

Tom was getting off the phone, crossing the room to her. "Are you all right?" he asked.

Slowly she dragged her eyes from the picture and looked up at him. She began to smile. "Tom, I'm feeling better than I have in a long time."

Tom smiled. "Then let's go home!"

TWENTY

The man sat at his desk in the clinic, having just dismissed a patient when an urgent phone call came in just before his lunch hour. He knew from the sound of his informer's voice there was trouble, but he was unprepared for the stunning news. Four people had linked him to the crime he had tried so hard to escape.

He stared into space. It was too late to run, too late to do anything more than call one of the best defense attorneys in the United States. He'd met him at a benefit in Washington last year. It would take millions to get him off, but money was all he had left, and he didn't really care anymore. The white powder had taken everything from him—his conscience, his pride, his dignity. There was nothing left.

He opened his desk drawer, thinking of the revolver he kept in the very back. The most sensible thing to do was to end it now, but something held him back. He could not say what.

He would go home and think. Maybe something would come to him. In the meantime, he would not give them the satisfaction of arresting him in front of his clients and his office staff.

In his dazed brain, he kept hearing the words of his mother, long dead, echoing. What a time to get religious! But then, what was left?

He had hit the pits. Maybe the lawyer could plead insanity.

James Maxwell Phillips was arrested at approximately two o'clock that afternoon. The man who had achieved fame as a brilliant psychiatrist was read his rights by two detectives while several policemen gathered on his front lawn.

"Before we ask you any questions, you must understand your rights. You have the right to remain silent. Anything you say can be used against you in court. You have the right to talk to a lawyer for advice before we ask you any questions and to have a lawyer with you during questioning. If you cannot afford a lawyer, one will be appointed for you before any questioning if you wish—"

Phillips sneered at that part.

"If you decide to answer questions now without a lawyer present, you will still have the right to stop answering at any time. You also have the right to stop answering at any time until you talk to a lawyer."

As the Miranda rights were recited to him, Phillips nodded, indicating that he understood, then said nothing.

His shocked housekeeping staff looked on in dismay as he was handcuffed and placed in the patrol car for his ride downtown. In the past, he would have hurled back some one-liner: *Take the day off!* Not now; not anymore. He was a broken man, and he didn't even care. He never said a word to the officers, to anyone.

When they arrived at the station, he looked dazedly past the hoards of reporters swarming like vultures. He went quietly and willingly, for in some part of his brain, there was an odd sense of relief. The hell that had been his life would soon be over.

Once again, Elizabeth and Michael sat in a small room with the detectives and the assistant DA, awaiting a lineup.

Phillips's arrest had been breaking news, and she had seen the same picture she had used to identify him staring back from the front page of the paper. She now knew about the cocaine habit. His drug supplier had been the one who kidnapped Tracy and had been nabbed at the Georgia-Alabama line and returned to Atlanta, along with a woman. Tracy was not pressing charges against the woman—she had been her friend, Tracy said. But the drug supplier had told everything to save himself, and so had Tony Laperra. Even the older woman whom everyone had feared would be of no help had declared she'd never forget that nose! All they needed to seal the charges against him was Elizabeth's testimony.

Her fingers were shaking as she reached for Michael's hand. His arm was around her shoulders, gently holding her, for he seemed to sense exactly what she was going through.

She took a deep breath, slowly releasing it, then another.

The door opened and six men crossed the stage. She slipped to the edge of the chair, staring wide-eyed through the mirrored wall. The men were instructed to turn to the right, giving her a profile of the left sides of their faces.

She gasped aloud. *It was him.* The second man from the right.

Dressed like the others in the orange uniform of prisoners, he still held himself erect, staring straight ahead, but behind the frameless glasses the eyes held a look of defeat.

Elizabeth's mouth was almost too dry to speak, but she began to nod her head as tears filled her eyes and flowed down her cheeks. For one horrible instant she was there again. She could feel the soft summer breeze on her face, experience the excitement of waiting for Michael for dinner, and then...

Then the black car had swerved around the side of the building. She had jumped out of her car, had run toward the Jaguar, running as fast as she could. She had to stop him from hitting the other car—she had to!

She was out of her seat screaming before Michael could grab her.

"It's him. He's the one who drove the Jaguar!"

"Take it easy, darling."

"He's the man," she said distinctly for everyone in the room to hear. "He's the man who ran over me, who hit the other car, who left the scene."

She covered her face with her hands, no longer able to look at the man who had brought so much misery to so many people. And yet, a prayer had been answered…they had found the man, she had identified him.

She wasn't quite sure what happened then, but somehow Michael gathered her in his arms and led her gently from the room, down a hall and outside where she could breathe fresh air.

"Oh, darling," he said, pulling her against his chest, "it's over now."

"The first part is over," she sobbed. "But there's still the trial."

"I don't think it will come to that," he said, smoothing her hair back from her face. "His attorney is already hinting at a plea bargain."

Elizabeth took a shaky breath and looked up at Michael. He was cupping her face with his hands, using his thumbs to wipe the tears from her lashes.

"Michael, I was thinking about something on the way back from Florida. All this suffering and misery everyone has experienced just can't be wasted; we have to find something constructive for someone."

"You're safe, your memory has returned, Tracy is fine…."

"I know. But I mean there has to be some good somehow to come out of this."

"Well," Michael drew a deep breath, "there's a rumor that Phillips may speak out against the cocaine addiction. I suppose that could be considered useful."

Elizabeth nodded slowly. Then she remembered what she had planned to do, what she knew she *must* do. She hadn't been sure that she could forgive the man enough to go through with her plan, but now she was certain.

She opened her purse and withdrew a pocket copy of Psalms, the same little book she gave to her clients.

"Will you see that he gets this? Tell him it's from me," she added, placing the Psalms carefully in Michael's hand.

At first Michael looked shocked; then slowly he began to shake his head, his eyes drifting skyward for a moment. "Why am I surprised? There isn't a mean bone in your body, is there?"

"As a matter of fact, there is. I want you to go back to work," she said, her brown eyes holding a twinkle once again.

"Go back to work?" he echoed.

"We're going to Angel Valley to search for a missing woman."

"We're going to do *what?*"

"When I was at Seascape, I heard of a missing woman up in Angel Valley. Maybe we could combine work and play. It could be a vacation."

"A vacation?" he echoed, staring down into her upturned face. He was already starting to grin, amused by her change of mood. He was so relieved to see her happy again. They were back to their old games and he loved it.

"Yes, you know I've been wanting to go to Angel Valley."

"Fine. But let's go home first."

"Okay." She heaved a deep sigh of relief as she stretched up to kiss his lips. "And this time it's really home."

Watch for *Spirits,* coming in October 1998

Elizabeth and Michael go to Angel Valley in the Smokies to find a missing person. There they become involved in a web of folklore and legend and a strange tale of spirits. In the process, they encounter a mysterious guide and a guardian angel who help them find the missing woman and teach them a thing or two about the Holy Spirit.

Dear Reader,

Writing this novel has been both the most challenging, yet in some ways the most rewarding, of all my books. About halfway through, the story started to write itself. I pray it turned out to your satisfaction.

I appreciate the way you've been so faithful to call, write, and continue to encourage me, and I thank you from the bottom of my heart.

Watch for *Spirits*, the final book in my continuing stories of Elizabeth and Michael, Jay and Tracy, and the rest of the Calloway family. I thought it appropriate that this adventure lead them back to Angel Valley, where my first publishing experience with Palisades began. The search for a missing person takes the Calloways deep into the Smokies where their handsome guide falls in love with a young mountain woman who is thought to be a guardian angel. It is a story of suspense and romance and fun...so meet me in Angel Valley.

Until then, to God be the glory!

Peggy Darty

You may write to Peggy Darty, c/o Multnomah Publishers, P.O. Box 1720, Sisters, Oregon 97759.

Palisades...Pure Romance

～ Palisades ～

Reunion, Karen Ball
Refuge, Lisa Tawn Bergren
Torchlight, Lisa Tawn Bergren
Treasure, Lisa Tawn Bergren
Chosen, Lisa Tawn Bergren
Firestorm, Lisa Tawn Bergren
Surrender, Lynn Bulock
Wise Man's House, Melody Carlson
Heartland Skies, Melody Carlson
Cherish, Constance Colson
Chase the Dream, Constance Colson
Angel Valley, Peggy Darty
Sundance, Peggy Darty
Moonglow, Peggy Darty
Promises, Peggy Darty
Memories, Peggy Darty
Remembering the Roses, Marion Duckworth (June 1998)
Love Song, Sharon Gillenwater
Antiques, Sharon Gillenwater
Texas Tender, Sharon Gillenwater
Secrets, Robin Jones Gunn
Whispers, Robin Jones Gunn
Echoes, Robin Jones Gunn
Sunsets, Robin Jones Gunn
Clouds, Robin Jones Gunn
Waterfalls, Robin Jones Gunn
Coming Home, Barbara Jean Hicks
Snow Swan, Barbara Jean Hicks
China Doll, Barbara Jean Hicks (June 1998)
Angel in the Senate, Kristen Johnson Ingram
Irish Eyes, Annie Jones

Father by Faith, Annie Jones
Irish Rogue, Annie Jones
Glory, Marilyn Kok
Sierra, Shari MacDonald
Forget-Me-Not, Shari MacDonald
Diamonds, Shari MacDonald
Stardust, Shari MacDonald
Westward, Amanda MacLean
Stonehaven, Amanda MacLean
Everlasting, Amanda MacLean
Kingdom Come, Amanda MacLean
Betrayed, Lorena McCourtney
Escape, Lorena McCourtney
Dear Silver, Lorena McCourtney
Forgotten, Lorena McCourtney
Enough! Gayle Roper
The Key, Gayle Roper
Voyage, Elaine Schulte

~ ANTHOLOGIES ~

A Christmas Joy, Darty, Gillenwater, MacLean
Mistletoe, Ball, Hicks, McCourtney
A Mother's Love, Bergren, Colson, MacLean
Silver Bells, Bergren, Krause, MacDonald
Heart's Delight, Ball, Hicks, Noble
Fools for Love, Ball, Brooks, Jones

THE PALISADES LINE

Look for these new releases at your local bookstore. If the title you seek is not in stock, the store may order you a copy using the ISBN listed.

Heartland Skies, Melody Carlson
ISBN 1-57673-264-9
Jayne Morgan moves to the small town of Paradise with the prospect of marriage, a new job, and plenty of horses to ride. But when her fiancé dumps her, she's left with loose ends. Then she wins a horse in a raffle, and the handsome rancher who boards her horse makes things look decidedly better.

Memories, Peggy Darty
ISBN 1-57673-171-5
In this sequel to *Promises,* Elizabeth Calloway is left with amnesia after witnessing a hit-and-run accident. Her husband, Michael, takes her on a vacation to Cancún so that she can relax and recover her memory. What they don't realize is that a killer is following them, hoping to wipe out Elizabeth's memory permanently....

Remembering the Roses, Marion Duckworth (June 1998)
ISBN 1-57673-236-3
Sammie Sternberg is trying to escape her memories of the man who betrayed her, and she ends up in a small town on the Olympic Peninsula in Washington. There she opens her dream business—an antique shop in an old Victorian—and meets a reclusive watercolor artist who helps to heal her broken heart.

Waterfalls, Robin Jones Gunn
ISBN 1-57673-221-5
In a visit to Glenbrooke, Oregon, Meredith Graham meets movie star Jacob Wilde and is sure he's the one. But when Meri puts her

foot in her mouth, things fall apart. Is isn't until the two of them get thrown together working on a book-and-movie project that Jacob realizes his true feelings, and this time he's the one who's starstruck.

China Doll, Barbara Jean Hicks (June 1998)
ISBN 1-57673-262-2
Bronson Bailey is having a mid-life crisis: after years of globetrotting in his journalism career, he's feeling restless. Georgine Nichols has also reached a turning point: after years of longing for a child, she's decided to adopt. The problem is, now she's fallen in love with Bronson, and he doesn't want a child.

Angel in the Senate, Kristen Johnson Ingram
ISBN 1-57673-263-0
Newly elected senator Megan Likely heads to Washington with high hopes for making a difference in government. But accusations of election fraud, two shocking murders, and threats on her life make the Senate take a backseat. She needs to find answers, but she's not sure who she can trust anymore.

Irish Rogue, Annie Jones
ISBN 1-57673-189-8
Michael Shaughnessy has paid the price for stealing a pot of gold, and now he's ready to make amends to the people he's hurt. Fiona O'Dea is number one on his list. The problem is, Fiona doesn't want to let Michael near enough to hurt her again. But before she knows it, he's taken his Irish charm and worked his way back into her life…and her heart.

Forgotten, Lorena McCourtney
ISBN 1-57673-222-3
A woman wakes up in an Oregon hospital with no memory of who she is. When she's identified as Kat Cavanaugh, she returns

to her home in California. As Kat struggles to recover her memory, she meets a fiancé she doesn't trust and an attractive neighbor who can't believe how she's changed. She begins to wonder if she's really Kat Cavanaugh, but if she isn't, what happened to the real Kat?

The Key, Gayle Roper
ISBN 1-57673-223-1
On Kristie Matthews's first day living on an Amish farm, she gets bitten by a dog and is rushed to the emergency room by a handsome stranger. In the ER, an elderly man in the throes of a heart attack hands her a key and tells her to keep it safe. Suddenly odd accidents begin to happen to her, but no one's giving her any answers.

⟶ ANTHOLOGIES ⟵

Fools for Love, Ball, Brooks, Jones
ISBN 1-57673-235-5
By Karen Ball: Kitty starts pet-sitting, but when her clients turn out to be more than she can handle, she enlists help from a handsome handyman.
By Jennifer Brooks: Caleb Murphy tries to acquire a book collection from a widow, but she has one condition: he must marry her granddaughter first.
By Annie Jones: A college professor who has been burned by love vows not to be fooled twice, until her ex-fiancé shows up and ruins her plans!

Heart's Delight, Ball, Hicks, Noble
ISBN 1-57673-220-7
By Karen Ball: Corie receives a Valentine's Day date from her sisters and thinks she's finally found the one…until she learns she went out with the wrong man.

By *Barbara Jean Hicks:* Carina and Reid are determined to break up their parents' romance, but when it looks like things are working, they have a change of heart.

By *Diane Noble:* Two elderly bird-watchers set aside their differences to try to save a park from disaster but learn they've bitten off more than they can chew.

BE SURE TO LOOK FOR ANY OF THE 1997 TITLES
YOU MAY HAVE MISSED:

Surrender, **Lynn Bulock** (ISBN 1-57673-104-9)
Single mom Cassie Neel accepts a blind date from her children for her birthday.

Wise Man's House, **Melody Carlson** (ISBN 1-57673-070-0)
A young widow buys her childhood dream house, and a mysterious stranger moves into her caretaker's cottage.

Moonglow, **Peggy Darty** (ISBN 1-57673-112-X)
Tracy Kosell comes back to Moonglow, Georgia, and investigates a case with a former schoolmate, who's now a detective.

Promises, **Peggy Darty** (ISBN 1-57673-149-9)
A Christian psychologist asks her detective husband to help her find a dangerous woman.

Texas Tender, **Sharon Gillenwater** (ISBN 1-57673-111-1)
Shelby Nolan inherits a watermelon farm and asks the sheriff for help when two elderly men begin digging holes in her fields.

Clouds, **Robin Jones Gunn** (ISBN 1-57673-113-8)
Flight attendant Shelly Graham runs into her old boyfriend, Jonathan Renfield, and learns he's engaged.

Sunsets, **Robin Jones Gunn** (ISBN 1-57673-103-0)
Alissa Benson has a run-in at work with Brad Phillips, and is more than a little upset when she finds out he's her neighbor!

Snow Swan, **Barbara Jean Hicks** (ISBN 1-57673-107-3)
Toni, an unwed mother and a recovering alcoholic, falls in love for the first time. But if Clark finds out the truth about her past, will he still love her?

Irish Eyes, **Annie Jones** (ISBN 1-57673-108-1)
Julia Reed gets drawn into a crime involving a pot of gold and has her life turned upside down by Interpol agent Cameron O'Dea.

Father by Faith, **Annie Jones** (ISBN 1-57673-117-0)
Nina Jackson buys a dude ranch and hires cowboy Clint Cooper as her foreman, but her son, Alex, thinks Clint is his new daddy!

Stardust, **Shari MacDonald** (ISBN 1-57673-109-X)
Gillian Spencer gets her dream assignment but is shocked to learn she must work with Maxwell Bishop, who once broke her heart.

Kingdom Come, **Amanda MacLean** (ISBN 1-57673-120-0)
Ivy Rose Clayborne, M.D., pairs up with the grandson of the coal baron to fight the mining company that is ravaging her town.

Dear Silver, **Lorena McCourtney** (ISBN 1-57673-110-3)
When Silver Sinclair receives a letter from Chris Bentley ending their relationship, she's shocked, since she's never met the man!

Enough! **Gayle Roper** (ISBN 1-57673-185-5)
When Molly Gregory gets fed up with her three teenaged children, she announces that she's going on strike.

A Mother's Love, **Bergren, Colson, MacLean**
(ISBN 1-57673-106-5)
Three heartwarming stories share the joy of a mother's love.

Silver Bells, **Bergren, Krause, MacDonald**
(ISBN 1-57673-119-7)
Three novellas focus on romance during Christmastime.